# The Pagan Writers' Guide

Writing for Pagan and
MB&S Publications

# The Pagan Writers' Guide

Writing for Pagan and
MB&S Publications

Mélusine Draco

**COMPASS
BOOKS**

Winchester, UK
Washington, USA

First published by Compass Books, 2013
Compass Books is an imprint of John Hunt Publishing Ltd., Laurel House, Station Approach,
Alresford, Hants, SO24 9JH, UK
office1@jhpbooks.net
www.johnhuntpublishing.com
www.compass-books.net

For distributor details and how to order please visit the 'Ordering' section on our website.

Text copyright: Mélusine Draco 2013

ISBN: 978 1 78279 108 9

A CIP catalogue record for this book is available from the British Library.

Design: Stuart Davies

Printed and bound by CPI Group (UK) Ltd, Croydon, CR0 4YY

We operate a distinctive and ethical publishing philosophy in all
areas of our business, from our global network of authors to
production and worldwide distribution.

# CONTENTS

# About the Author

Writing as Mélusine Draco, the author has published over 30 books on esoteric subjects, particularly about the Egyptian Mystery Tradition and traditional British Old Craft, in addition to being a contributor to a wide range of pagan magazines such as *The Cauldron, Prediction, Pentacle, Brigid's Fire* (Ireland) and *Witches & Pagans* (USA), and currently writing for Moon Books and Axis Mundi imprints of John Hunt Publishing. Under her real name of Suzanne Ruthven she has been editor of *The New Writer* since 1994; contributor for a wide range of publications as diverse as *The Lady, Country Illustrated, The Countryman* and *The Funeral Director's Journal*; ten years as commissioning editor for ignotus press; and now commissioning editor for Compass Books. **www.facebook.com/JHPCompassBooks**

Chapter One

# In The Beginning There Was The Word

*'I want to be a pagan author and write for the pagan community'* ...
*'Can you tell me how to get published?'*

Two separate postings on the Internet suggested that pagan writing has finally moved from the 'hidden' into mainstream where readers are becoming more circumspect in their choice of material; and that it was time to produce a serious guide for would-be pagan writers. Firstly, in answer to the blog posting, writing for the pagan community is no different from writing for any other readership – so we need to learn the basic rules before deciding whether we have any talent worth pursuing. After that, it will depend on the level of our own expertise as to whether anyone will look favourably on our submissions.

Pagan publishing has now spread across the world and there is no shortage of opportunities for writers, whether it be in print or on-line. The pagan voice is 'heard on every wind' and there are markets everywhere in the English-speaking world. The on-line community spreads the word to the furthest reaches of the globe, and book reviews give pagan authors far more coverage than they could have generated in years of traditional marketing.

One mainstream review was in response to *Traditional Witchcraft for the Seashore* and the second posting – on Andy Lloyd's Book Reviews – suggested there might be an opening for a serious guide. 'The learning is multi-disciplinary, and feels almost as if one is studying a textbook written by a poet. Yet the science collated in these pages is interesting and pragmatic,' wrote the kindly Mr Lloyd. 'Intermingled with the factual information is much about rituals, superstitions, beach treasures to collect for magical means and, of course, spell-casting.'

Generally speaking, today's paganism falls into four different elements, which in turn separates the different approaches and levels of magical practice, and subsequently, the writing. Each category requires that it should be written for, and read by, followers at that level of 'learning' to avoid any misunderstandings. A considerable amount of magical writing can be incomprehensible to those who have not been schooled in that particular path or tradition – so we begin at the beginning and work ourselves up through the spheres of **Knowledge, Wisdom** and **Understanding**. And we start by accepting that there *is* a divide between the various approaches to paganism and magical practice.

- **Animistic:** The belief that everything animate and inanimate has its own life force, such as that which forms the basis of shamanism, Shinto, Aboriginal, Native American, etc.,
- **Eclectic:** Selecting or borrowing from a variety of styles, systems, theories, beliefs, etc., as commonly found in modern paganism and Wicca.
- **Syncretic:** The attempt to reconcile different systems of belief; the fusion or blending of religions, as by identification of gods, taking over of observances, or selection of whatever seems best in each; often producing a seemingly illogical compromise in belief. This approach is found in many aspects of Western Ritual Magic, and the initiatory branches of the European and British esoteric groups.
- **Synergetic:** Combined or co-ordinated action; increased effect of two elements obtained by using them together. The combining of ancient wisdom with modern magical applications, as in the case of the Egyptian Mystery Tradition, Old Craft, the Norse traditions and Druidism.

Regardless of our own personal levels of esoteric learning, we need to go back to the basics of creative writing and see what tricks of the trade we can utilise. We will see why editors and publishers are inundated with submissions of a certain kind – and what we can do to give our writing 'editor appeal'. We will learn how to develop ideas via lateral thinking, and develop the art of 'seeing' through an editor's eyes, i.e. visualisation.

## Back To Basics

How many times do we read (or heed) the advice about hooking an editor's attention? How many writers fail to appreciate that if the editor (or publisher) isn't hooked right from the start our submission *will* be rejected? And it doesn't matter whether we are talking about non-fiction or fiction, short stories or novels, poetry or prose – it must have something to make the reader want to turn the page. If it fails to entice in the opening sentences, then we will be lucky if the professional reader even bothers to go to the next paragraph.

## Exercise

### What exactly is a hook?

It is a simple device for introducing our subject with impact, rather than long-winded preamble. That opening line or first paragraph is the most important part of the whole piece. It may be a challenging statement. A question. Brilliant use of language or analogy. Evocative description of a person, place or thing. And it doesn't matter how brilliant the rest of our work may be – an editor isn't even going to read it unless we've hooked their attention right from the start.

Our first exercise is to study a selection of pagan magazines. We may already subscribe to one or more; in which case we will be familiar with the differences in house-style. Begin by reading the editorial and any submission guidelines – these are included in the magazine, or found on the website – and make notes about the type of material in each publication. Into which categories do the majority of these subjects fall? Divination ... herb craft ... Tarot ... astrology ... healing ...crystals ...witchcraft ... magic? **Which of these are *your* favourite subjects – and the one *you* know most about?**

Now check the opening lines of each article and see how each writer has introduced their subject. Is it with a bang – or a whimper? Are the title and sub-title eye-catching? Do they make strong, bold statements to introduce the topic, or paint a subtler picture? Is there a clear indication of what the article is about? Make a note of those beginnings you find striking ... and those that don't raise any interest at all. Now try writing a few introductions – one or two sentences – to your favourite subject, while we have a quick look how pagan publishing has evolved.

## In The Beginning ...

Things were in the past a lot different with pagan or esoteric publishing. There were no glossy subscription magazines, although *Psychic News* (1932) and *Prediction* (1936) magazines could be found on the top shelf at the larger newsagents. The 1960s and 70s saw an embryonic sub-culture of esoteric magazines and newsletters begin to flourish as underground presses, including *The Wiccan* (1969), which later became *Pagan Dawn* (journal of the Pagan Federation), with *The Cauldron*, edited by Michael Howard, and the *Fortean Times* seeing the light of day in 1976.

But it was the *Lamp of Thoth,* edited by Chris Bray of the Sorcerer's Apprentice that for me conjures up fond memories and nostalgia for those 'bad old days'. LOT was published throughout the 1980s and it was via its pages many of us 'gained access to the wider world of the British occult scene' as Phil Hine wrote recently – he later began publishing *Pagan News* in the late 1980s.

There are a few of us who can remember the Gestetner, a

stencil-duplicating machine; the first piece of office equipment to produce numerous copies of documents quickly and inexpensively ... and barely decipherably. The majority of pagan publications were produced by this means, which probably accounts for the defective eyesight of the old brigade! There were dozens of different publications produced at secret addresses, and it was a magical quest in itself tracking down those we wanted to read. As the era of desk-top publishing dawned, the production methods improved and, by the mid 1990s, the remaining titles evolved into professionally produced independent magazines such as *Pentacle* and *The Cauldron*.

One thing that has never changed, however, is these have always been non-paying markets, with individual contributors supporting them because of their commitment to the Old Ways, and the preservation of esoteric knowledge and traditions. As far as the would-be pagan writer is concerned, this is hardly likely to change – simply because the most well known authors are perfectly willing to submit material without a fee and will continue to do so. Because these magazines are non-paying, it should not be thought they are in any way inferior since those long-standing members of the pagan community judge the content more critically than would a more commercial readership.

For new writers, *Pagan Dawn* and *Pentacle* are the places to 'cut the writing teeth' because they offer the best introduction to the world of publishing that often straddles the pagan and 'mind, body and spirit' genres. Read these magazines regularly and it helps us discover what's what and who's who in the pagan book and magazine world – and this exercise should be viewed as serving an apprenticeship before attempting to move to paying outlets.

## Positive Mental Attitude

Once a writer crosses that great divide between writing for profit rather than pleasure, there are certain realities that need to be taken into account. Twenty years ago, the world of pagan writing provided hundreds of outlets for writers with varying levels of talent. There were opportunities galore for even the most mediocre. All this has changed and even the amateur freelance now needs a highly professional approach if they wish to succeed in an extremely competitive industry.

In other words, we need to develop PMA (positive mental attitude) when it comes to writing because this requires a process of conditioning. Unfortunately, many tutors still foster the myth that *everyone* can be taught to write professionally and profitably – this is not so. As a parallel, you might manage a nifty round of golf, but it doesn't mean you're destined for the Ryder Cup; you may achieve something in the local club event – but it's *not* Gleneagles. PMA demands that we analyse our own abilities and what we can realistically achieve. Reading about writing, attending workshops and subscribing to magazines does not make you a writer. **Publication does – especially if it's paid and on a regular basis.**

Having confidence in our own ability helps. So does understanding the basics of researching the markets; to grasp where *we* see ourselves fitting into the scheme of things. We also discover that those writing for fun and those writing for financial reward speak a different language, viewing the situation from a different perspective. People write for all sorts of reasons – and all of them valid – but the process of developing PMA towards the craft of writing means that we've got to choose between competing with the winners – or just talking with the also-rans.

The point often made about those 'scratching a living' from writing isn't exaggeration. Most freelances waste more time trying to drum up living expenses than they do writing. In fact, they need a *stronger* sense of PMA than those writing purely for pleasure. A serious writer cannot afford *not* to develop PMA if they are to survive in a competitive environment.

## How can we define PMA?

Ambition or aspiration, perhaps. For either the writer still needs an extra ingredient – which can be more accurately described as 'the strength to dream'. As we get older, we lose the ability to hold onto a dream; life's disappointments knock the stuffing out of us, and our dreams turn to dust. Without ambition, without a dream, without positive mental attitude, any writer will struggle against the tide.

The majority of writers experience their first successes among what was at one time referred to as the 'small presses' – independent, sole-participant publications, but again the value of this marketplace should never be undervalued. But the day *will* come when you have to make the decision to break out and aim for mainstream publication. If you are content to remain with the 'one man and his dog' operation, fine, but don't criticise those who decide to aim higher. Over the years there have been some exceptional writers whose capabilities suggested greater things but because of a lack of PMA, they remained within the small presses, rather than risk rejection in a more challenging arena.

- Positive mental attitude gives us the ability to access our own strengths and weaknesses.
- It refuses to allow us to be precious about our own writing because if it's *that* good why isn't it selling?
- It prevents us from convincing ourselves that an editor is an idiot because they haven't seen the point. If the editor hasn't seen it, it's because we haven't made it clearly enough.
- It encourages us to compare our writing to that published in the various magazines where we would like to see our by-line appear.
- It prevents us from setting our goals too high because this can quickly lead to disillusionment.

• And it helps us to face the fact that rejection slips *will* come.

The bulk of pagan writing is non-fiction and everyone has some aspect of their life that can be worked into a publishable article, so let's see if we can learn a few of those tricks of the trade. Non-fiction isn't an easy way out; it has all the quirks of fiction writing and then some ... What it *does* provide is the discipline for writing, economy of language, the cut and thrust of submission and rejection, a higher rate of acceptances – and it pays better, too. And, while this is going on, you can still work on your novel, short stories and poetry, because mastering fiction writing can add that extra zest to brighten up the dullest fact in non-fiction. The best way of developing PMA is to get to know and under-stand ourselves – and who knows where it will lead if we retain the strength to dream.

## Fiction and Verse – Earth, Air, Fire and Water

There is a dearth of outlets for pagan fiction, but hopefully this is gradually changing. If we go to the Moon Books Facebook page, we can see that there has been a long-running debate about the possibility of including pagan fiction and poetry despite the fact that this will probably *not* be a money-spinner for the publisher. As a compromise, publisher Trevor Greenfield has introduced 'subsidy' fiction (see Interview in Chapter Four) along the lines of the highly successful Troubador/Matador scheme; and is consid-ering the addition of a 'poetry page' to the Moon Books blog.

Esoteric fiction has been around for a long time and is respon-sible for encouraging further exploration into the (then) hidden realms of witchcraft and ritual magic by genuine seekers after enlightenment. The most popular author being Dion Fortune, whose series of novels managed to impart sufficient information to set thousands on the quest for *The Demon Lover, The Winged Bull, The Sea-Priestess, Moon Magic* and *The Goat-Foot God*. Just as intriguing but less known were Aleister Crowley's *Moon Child* (originally *The Butterfly Net*) and *The Scrutinies of Simon Iff.*

Esoteric fiction differs from horror and fantasy in that it is based on genuine magical 'truths'. It shouldn't just 'suspend disbelief' – it needs to draw the reader into the 'hidden' world to such a degree that there is realisation of what genuine magic is all about – if we can only find the key. The fiction of American author H P Lovecraft, for example, gave birth to a whole new cult, based on some 'fifty-three stories and assorted fragments ... all of which are based upon a bizarre and terrifying occult mythology.' Originally written for the cheap pulp horror magazines of his time (1890-1937), they have subsequently gained a reputation for having genuinely powerful occult significance.

By contrast, Arthur Machen, regarded as one of the finest of Welsh mystical writers, *was* for a short time a member of the Order of the Golden Dawn, although most of his best stories have a 'hint of pantheist mystery about them, and are far away from the theatre of ritual'. His most popular works include *The Great God Pan* (1890), *The Hill of Dreams* (1895) and *The Three Imposters* (1895).

Good esoteric fiction doesn't rely on shock tactics to enthral the reader; it is the dripping of *genuine* occult lore into the story, so that the lines become blurred between fact and fiction, that matters. If the pagan reader is aware of glaring errors, then the story loses its power, although non-pagans will hardly be aware of the underlying occult significance. For example, this short story was originally written for the Canongate Prize with the theme of 'Sinning', but as that publishing house has more than a little Christian bias, it's not surprising it didn't find favour with the judges. The story was later accepted for publication by *Dark Fiction* magazine and *The New Writer* ... and contains quite a few 'truths' for the unsuspecting reader.

*More Sinned Against ...*

**Freelance journalist Suzanne Ruthven shakes hands with the Devil in the most unlikely of circumstances.**

You don't expect the Devil to turn up for an interview wearing Gucci loafers, jeans and a T-shirt. It comes as even more of a shock to discover that this tall, blond man with the imperious manner is a far cry from the creature of nightmare I'd been expecting. His whole being exudes a striking presence as his handsome, angular features change from kindly to predatory, and back again. Without even turning to look, he knows that everyone in the room is watching him.

This is Lucifer, the morning star, the 'fallen' angel and light-bearer (which is what his names mean), and we're here to discuss his autobiography, *More Sinned Against...* that has catapulted into the best-selling lists in less than two weeks, and has been hailed as a 21st century publishing phenomena by Book-Watch.

'Milton was the first to give me a sympathetic hearing,' he says with a wry, knowing smile. 'He portrayed me as wicked, but as we well know, the worse the rogue, the greater his magnetism. Milton's own private life throws some questionable shadow on his *own* character but he obviously realised, like all commercial writers, that vice sells more than virtue.'

Lucifer is obviously not unkindly disposed towards the 'factional' portrayal in *Paradise Lost*. John Milton's archfiend is so magnificently proud, so full of courage, eloquence and arrogant defiance, that the 'loyal' angels of heaven pale into insignificance beside the flamboyant anti-hero. But just how much of the story is based on fact?

'It was an unauthorised biography and a lot of it was made up purely to fill space,' he replies. 'Although for the time it was certainly *avant-garde*. I doubt whether he originally intended me to overshadow the rest of the company but the archangels finished up pathetically neuter by comparison. Michael never forgave me, but then he always was a humourless bastard.'

Perhaps Milton realised his error in making Lucifer too great in *Paradise Lost*, for in a later work, *Samson Agonistes*, he is less awesome and has lost much of the size and dignity that both attracted and repelled the reader. Lucifer raises a perfectly formed eyebrow.

'*That*, I suspect was Michael's doing. Milton obviously had a lot of empathy with what *he* saw as me. Although in his public life he was known as a 'champion of chastity and marital constancy', his writing reveals some less than pure fantasies.'

Is he suggesting that Michael Archangel leant on John Milton, applying 'some celestial muscle' in order to change the emphasis of his writing? A waitress brings our drinks and Lucifer turns to her with a smile of such high-voltage radiance that for a moment she's mesmerised. The rapt expression shows that he's only to crook his little finger and she'd follow him to hell and back. Lucifer turns his attention back to the question and the radiance dims; the girl walks away in a daze – she's been tempted by a glimpse of paradise and was, for a moment, lost.

'Shall we say there was a certain muddying of the waters,' he replies carefully but without a trace of rancour. 'Somewhere along the line my name became confused with some petty legal official, called a 'satan', whose business it was to poke and pry into people's cupboards and rattle a few skeletons. This insidious little creature's function was to test man's fidelity to God by offering certain temptations and, whilst not the sort of person one would cultivate socially, it was not an *evil* entity.'

So, how *did* the Light-bearer become the Prince of Darkness? *More Sinned Against ...* is a story of dark political intrigue set against a background of emerging nations and the struggle for both spiritual and temporal power. Not just revelations about the androgynous bitchiness prevalent amongst the Heavenly Host – this is a hard-hitting, fast-moving account of how ecclesiastical history was rewritten in order to provide a scapegoat for all that was wrong in the world.

First and foremost, as the book is quick to point out, is the marked difference between Lucifer and 'satan'. In Christian terms, 'Satan' eventually came to personify everything that is evil, corrupt and depraved; he tempts mankind with rich rewards in exchange for man's immortal soul. Dr Rossell Hope Robbins, an expert on demonology, maintained that this 'satan' was merely the creation of incompetent clerics who bungled the translation of the Old Testament into Greek. In this case, the expulsion from Heaven wasn't due to any fall from grace, but rather a slip of the pen.

Lucifer's own antecedents are much more impressive. Some Gnostic sects regard him as a divine power in his own right, or even as the first-born son of God. His lineage can certainly be traced all the way back to the Semitic cultures of the Euphrates and Tigris Basin – long before the Israelites began to settle in Palestine. The Romans identified him with the planet Venus as it appears just before sunrise, while in Tuscan folklore it was believed Lucifer was the brother of Diana, goddess of hunting and the moon.

With this amount of clout behind him, it's more than surprising that Lucifer became *persona non grata* as, far as Heaven was concerned. His sin must have been pretty horrendous to warrant such a violent and unrelenting expulsion, I venture. Idly, his long, tapering fingers smooth the fabric of his jeans and he's clearly embarrassed by the question. We are interrupted by the waitress refreshing our drinks but Lucifer is preoccupied and she turns away, obviously disappointed that she has not been the focus of his brilliant smile.

'I had the audacity to interfere with evolution in order to accelerate the development of mankind,' he finally answers in a soft voice. 'I gave man knowledge and for this perceived sin I was unceremoniously 'cast out of heaven'. Adam would probably still be mooching around in that damned garden if I hadn't given Eve the apple. He was a pretty dismal creature for something made in the image of God. His first wife left him, you know.'

Now we're getting to the reason why *More Sinned Against* ... has been so successful. This is the drugs, sex and rock n' roll of the Bible and Lucifer doesn't pull any punches with his revelations. Over the years his name's been linked with the most beautiful women in the world, and although he's spared *their* blushes, he's not been so charitable towards their men folk. Is it true that he gave Eve more than an apple?

His eyes glitter dangerously as a slightly malicious smile hovers on his lips. 'Let's just say that revenge is a dish best served cold and Adam was hardly at home in those days. He was running around trying to impress everyone with his newly acquired knowledge. Hell's teeth! That man could bore for Paradise! And in the bedroom stakes he was far from omnipotent, I can tell you. Eve was pretty miffed because it had been her who took the apple and now Adam was pretending it was all his own idea. She wanted to get her own back.'

Natural female curiosity and professional journalism tumble over each other with the desire to know what Eve was really like. She was, after all, the *first* woman. Surely she'd got to be a bit special? Lucifer throws back his head in laughter, revealing pearly white teeth and a slightly wolfish cast to his features. He knows why I'm asking and is amused by this descent of professional concentration into vulgar inquisition.

'Actually, she was plain and rather stupid by design. You must remember that Lilith, Adam's first wife, was a real looker, a firebrand, and in order not to make the same mistake again, it was decided that poor Eve shouldn't be blessed with the same attributes. She couldn't be, of course, because Lilith was one of the immortals and Eve was only human – and made from Adam's rib to boot!'

The popular mythos maintains that Lilith was rejected by Adam, rather than the other way about. Lucifer's amber eyes gleam like the morning star: part wolf, part cat, part goat. He snorts in response. 'She considered herself – quite rightly – equal if not superior to Adam and objected to adopting the so-called missionary position during their conjugal coupling. When Adam tried to enforce his masculine superiority, she decamped from their marital lair to lodge a complaint with the Creation Department.

'Unfortunately, the prototype had been approved and they weren't going to alter it merely to please some chit of a girl, immortal or not, so she was told to either like it or lump it. As a result she went off on a jaunt with ... shall we say, a more *appreciative* companion.

'Adam complained, as usual, and Michael sent three of his celestial 'heavies' to fetch her back but Lilith refused point blank to return to the poor specimen Creation had furnished for her. They were forced to supply a more compliant Eve by way of a compromise and to shut Adam up. It set the programme back so far that they had to throw in another Ice Age as a cover-up for Creation's mismanagement.'

We were sailing into dangerous waters. *More Sinned Against ...* originally ran into censorship problems because of what was seen as indelicate references to who really begat whom in the Biblical sense. After two thousand years of misrepresentation, the lid was finally coming off the cauldron with a fine head of sulphuric steam.

Lucifer's name has often been linked with Lilith and they do have the same Semitic ancestry. Some said she was his daughter in order to compound the sin of incest. Others claim she was his mistress and that between them they spawned a whole motley assortment of off-spring. One of these fascinating creatures being brought home from Jerusalem by an early Count of Anjou; from their union came the Angevin line from whom our present Royal Family can claim descent. So it's not difficult to see how the political ramifications of his allegations have upset the Establishment.

'This divine cock-up resulted in the emergence of two separate bloodlines in the human race,' Lucifer explains, choosing his words very carefully – but not without a certain relish. 'Those descending from Adam who have been successfully held in check by monotheism; and those descending from Cain, who were the carriers of esoteric knowledge and great learning.'

But surely Cain was the first murderer!?

'It depends on who writes the script,' says Lucifer, scorn showing openly in his voice for the first time. 'Did Cain kill his brother, or was it an accident – or even a legitimate tribal sacrifice? Penalties in those days were pretty severe and yet all that happened to Cain was that he was 'cast out' from the tribe with the proviso that no one should kill him. Does that sound like a 'guilty' verdict to you?

'Cain's descendents represent a long line of seekers after truth, they became magicians, mystics, alchemists, scholars – anyone who was not bound by the decree that knowledge was sinful. The Burning Times wasn't about ridding the world of evil, it was a last ditch attempt to prevent the spread of learning.'

Yes, the political ramifications of such subversive thinking are frightening. In the present climate of an ego-centric society, *More Sinned Against* ... could open the flood-gates of revolution. Lucifer himself knows a thing or two about the repercussions of such violence. Several of his own children have suffered as a result and he's not about to let it happen again without fighting back. This time, however, he's using the pen not a flaming sword, pestilence, famine or plague.

Supported by the writings of modern esotericist, Rudolf Steiner, Lucifer is seen as the means by which man can be lifted upwards into the realms of light. According to Steiner, he 'breathes into man [or woman] the wonderful ability to aspire towards the spiritual realm. And to wrest free from the earth-embedding clutches of nature (which is not man's proper home) ...' This doctrine does, however, warn of Lucifer's tendency to excess, in that he would free man from his earthly toils and encourage him to abandon the responsibility for the regeneration of the earth.

'This is the *real* battle I have with Michael Archangel,' Lucifer explains, his good nature firmly back in place at the mention of his old adversary. 'Left to him, no one would be allowed to aspire to the spiritual realms until after they were dead. He'll battle for a soul like a rat over a crust but he will not assist anyone to elevate themselves intellectually or spiritually on this level of existence. Personally, I think it shows signs of a serious insecurity problem.'

So why has he waited until now to attempt to put his side of the story? 'Because until now, no publisher would touch the book. And after two thousand years of slander and libel, I think it's a good time as any to hit back. *Times they are a-changin'*, as Bob Dylan wrote. There isn't any theologian who can support any of the accusations that have been levelled against me. They have nothing to substantiate their claims, and I knew they wouldn't risk going to court to get the book suppressed since the attendant publicity would have been solely to *my* advantage.'

It's true. The name Lucifer appears only once in holy

scripture, as a translation of the Hebrew *heilet* (Isaiah, 14:12), which means 'spreading brightness'. The Latin *lucifer* means 'carrier of fire' and the Greek equivalent *phosphoros* has much the same meaning. But can his version be believed – after all this Prince of Light is also known as the Prince of Liars – but reading the book does raise some serious doubts. Is he really *More Sinned Against ...* than sinning?

'I look upon myself as one of the good guys,' he confides with a laugh. He stands, signalling that the interview is at an end and extends his hand.

I shake hands with the Devil and thank him for his time. It's all very civilized. He turns and walks away, surrounded by a shimmering aura of light. As every head turns to watch him I'm left with the impression that, despite all the difficulties, it really was preferable to reign in hell than serve in heaven.

**Read his story and judge for yourself ...**

Although a modern concept of the genre, this example uses all the devices that were employed by Machen, Fortune and Crowley to convey real 'magical truths' that are obvious to the initiate but obscure to the lay-reader. How many *genuine* esoteric references can you spot in the text?

Pagan poetry, with its penchant for analogy and metaphor can also appeal to a much wider readership as Robin Skelton and Margaret Blackwood's anthology, *Earth, Air, Fire, Water* demonstrated. This collection of British songs, rhymes and ballads with its pre-Christian and pagan elements, drew on traditional sources such as Mother Goose and the 17th century poems of Robert Herrick. As with all fields of poetry, however, and despite its popularity with poets and readers, few people actually will actually *buy* volumes of contemporary poetry. This means it is not financially viable for publishers to include poetry collections on their titles list, and the major outlets for pagan poets are the editors of pagan magazines who may, or may not, be too discerning about what they accept for publication.

To demonstrate the versatility of pagan-themed poetry, the following set of three poems was accepted by Abigail Morley, Poetry Editor of *The New Writer*, a mainstream publication for creative writers ...

### Witch I
I am a Woman Cats Run To

Toads roll over, offer me their soft bellies,
bats swoop down to plait my wayward hair
and spiders' silk binds up my wounds.
I cultivate my warts, grow fungi in damp places,
and in the light of a full moon, the silver slime
of slugs and snails glistens on my skin –
keeps me always, ever young. Newts leap and
splash at my approach. While I munch chestnuts
from my chestnut tree, my fire burns.
The cauldron steams with potent potions,
alchemical lotions to reassemble lizard,
make the blind worms see and grow the grass
in pavement cracks. The fox barks and I bark back.
When the wraiths pass me in the day,
Warn their children to keep away, I chuckle.

### Witch II
Me they would have hung,
led me up the stairs,
to the trapdoor and the rope,
watched with eager eyes,
as my neck snapped.

Me they would have pricked

to see if I could bleed,
searched for marks of concourse
with the devil,
left upon my skin at birth.

Me they would have swum,
thrown into the local pond,
while all the village gathered round
to see if I would drown,
and if I did, perhaps one or two,
would say as the final bubbles
broke the surface
that really I was not that bad.

Or if I managed to survive,
taking me sopping to a local tree
and string me up –
sure now of my witchery.

Me they would have burned,
piled the green sticks in a pyre
to make the fire burn longer
and tied me to the stake,
told their daughters to look at me
and learn from my mistakes.

*Witch III*
They threw me in. I held my tongue,
Would give none of them the satisfaction,
felt the cold burn into me and the dank
slime of the pond, its putrefaction,
the first forewarning of the grave to come.
The water closed above my head,
their jeering ceased and down I sank,

my skirts a swirl of storm-tossed leaves.
I never thought the pond so deep.
Light lessened, vanished and the dark was
quiet. I let myself sink down and down
and came to rest among the silt and mud,
pond bed, pillow soft. I waited,
breathed through gills that had appeared
when needed. Two toads I knew,
approached like cats, one to sit upon my lap,
one to stand guard and watch.
Far, far above, the sunlight played its distant
theme of flower-filled meadows, human cruelty.
Night fell. The blacky depths were velvet
on my skin but it was time. I stirred myself.
The toads moved off, to do their toad-like things.
I floated up and broke the surface,
felt once again the burning cold.
Houses around the pond
were shuttered tight. Few lights burned
but others had gone early
to bed that night, put an end
to the day, for people do not always say
what they think when there's a crowd
this will gnaw away at them.
They only have themselves to blame.
I found the shallows, stood on firmer
ground and the dogs began to bark with fear.
**Emer Gillespie**

Commenting on her selection, Abigail Morley said: 'I chose Emer Gillespie's poems because they are beautifully formed, linguistically vibrant and have an earthiness about them. They are bold poems that use the metaphor of witchcraft to give the poet an opportunity to make a comment about herself and her place in the world. I don't see them as 'pagan' poems, but as poems inspired by pagan mythology, and having them in a mainstream magazine is perfectly acceptable. The important thing is the way they are crafted and the story they tell.'

## Mind, Body and Spirit

The 'mind, body and spirit' genre is one of the non-fiction 'boom' categories that is destined to grow judging from the number of new titles appearing in the publishers' catalogues and the new magazines that have sprung up in recent years. But what exactly is mind, body and spirit – or MB&S for short?

- In a nutshell, any traditional subject that encompasses old concepts of teaching updated so that the *layperson* has instant access to ancient wisdom.
- Traditional learning linked to New Age psychology and therapy to offer a key to personal self-help and improvement for a non-pagan reader.
- Alternative health and fitness regimes to improve the quality of daily living.
- Westernised Oriental philosophies utilising relaxation and harmony techniques without the need for in-depth study.

Unlike publications on witchcraft, magic and paganism, which were in the past only available from specialist bookshops – couched in esoteric jargon that added to the mystery and confusion – those dealing with MB&S subjects had a higher degree of 'respectability'. The reader didn't have to be pagan to be interested in alternative therapies. Much of this has changed since the publishing industry recognised a vast market potential in self-improvement and spirituality for the masses. Although the articles tend to be written from a non-magico-religious perspective, there are the occasional 'white witchcraft' columns that serve to demonstrate the open-mindedness of the commissioning editor.

MB&S covers a wide range of topics common to pagan writing and therefore requires a diverse stable of writers to meet the supply and demand. The topics fall roughly into the following categories and although the authors are usually listed as psycho- and dream-therapists, healers, counsellors, teachers, psychics, etc., this should not discourage anyone of pagan persuasion with working experience in these fields from submitting a proposal.

## Health and Healing

Breathing and movement exercises; reflexology and chakra control; herbal remedies and aromatherapy; acupressure; creating perfumes; alternative choices in healing; channelling healing energies; shiatsu; self-healing; homeopathic medicine; creating sacred space with feng shui; Chinese herbal medicine; how to awaken and develop healing potential; iridology; massage; complimentary medicine; Chinese systems of food cures; gypsy folk medicine; Irish cures and superstitions; Tai Chi; flower remedies; yoga; Bach flower therapy; reiki; healthy eating, etc.

## Divination

Using dreams and the Tarot to determine the future; moon, star and sun signs; the power of gems and crystals; Chinese elemental astrology; predictive astrology; lovers' horoscopes; palmistry; Chinese and Aztec astrology; handwriting secrets revealed; rune magic; tree wisdom; dictionaries for dreams, superstitions, etc.

## Self-Help and Improvement

Developing the inner-self; psycho-regression; the power of inner peace; meditation techniques; sexual dreaming; how to attract money; the I-Ching; using colour to reflect holistic being; neuro-linguistic programming; the art of sexual magic; development of the personality; transcendental meditation, etc.,

## Spirituality

Using a psycho-spiritual approach to everyday life; practical guides to shamanism; how to develop psychic power; karma and reincarnation; supernatural sites; pre-death experiences and the after-life; spiritual healing; care of the soul; psychic protection; cosmic consciousness, etc.,

## Folklore and Mythology

This category includes every form of Celtic influence, not to mention obscure topics such as Aboriginal mythology, and a wealth of superstition and folklore from all over the world.

As we can see, there are few subjects that *don't* fall into the MB&S genre. The secret is to fully understand what is currently on offer and even more important – **the level from which the subject is being approached by individual publishers**. Many esoteric topics take years of learning before we even scratch the surface, so writing for the layperson means that the subject must be couched in layperson's language. The secret of MB&S writing is the author's ability to make the practice of their chosen subject appear easy to follow or achieve. A publisher will reject writing that goes over the heads of a general readership because the treatment is judged to be *too* esoteric or specialised.

As an example of a well-balanced MB&S title, without any pagan associations (although astrology also plays an important part in pagan belief), let's look at Jonathan Cainer's *Guide to the Zodiac*. Firstly, he has excellent credentials having written astrology columns for *Woman*, *Prima* and *Woman & Home*, *The Daily Express*, *The Mirror* plus magazines in USA and Australia. He is resident astrologer for *The Daily Mail* and although not many of us would be able to match such glowing antecedents, we will need to state why we are qualified to write about our subject and produce some background information to support our claims.

Most people know which 'star' or sun sign they were born under even if they don't glance at the daily horoscope in the newspaper. Jonathan Cainer gives a gentle, non-patronising introduction to his subject and then takes the reader right back to basics – even debunking the myth about 'being born on the cusp'. According to the author this is 'an artificial invention, created to cover up the fact that the zodiac signs don't conveniently click over at midnight on a particular date.' This little piece of throw away information immediately offers the essential 'hook' that shows this chap knows what he's talking about – and the budding astrologer wants to discover what other surprises are in store. Each sign also has 'real-life' examples of how the particular signs react to each other and in certain everyday situations. In the second part the author examines the individual moon signs and the influence each phase has on the day, place and time of birth. This is usually the deeper aspect of astrological writing but Jonathan Cainer maintains a light and easy approach that is also entertaining since this is where he slips in his 'history of astrology in two pages'.

As we can see, this is an extremely well-balanced approach to a popular subject, but what happens if we want to tackle something that is less familiar. Chris Sempers, editor of Corvus Books' 'Magical World' series is quite definite about the differences between writing for a specifically targeted readership and mainstream publications.

Take writing about crystals, for example. Corvus is looking **for magical material for magical practitioners**, so we're not particularly interested in the mind, body and spirit approach. Mainstream publishers mostly require a lighter treatment on crystal healing or divination and usually steer well clear of the magical aspects. Even so, it still requires a broad knowledge about the propensities of individual crystals and what they can be used for. All these subjects stem from ancient lineage and I believe it's important not to trivialise them purely for monetary gain.

These sentiments echoed my own feelings when writing *Magic Crystals, Sacred Stones* for Axis Mundi Books. The result is a book that is aimed at those who have explored crystal working as a beginner and who now wish to understand the mysteries of the Earth at a deeper level. Although it echoes the ancient beliefs in the magic surrounding gemstones and crystals, it is a book that will not compromise anyone who might otherwise shy away from what they would normally perceive as 'pagan writing'.

These subjects also find a growing range of outlets among the mainstream women's magazines aimed at the 20-40s age group. Study a selection of material from the mini-snippets in the weeklies, to full-length features in the monthlies and you're sure to find at least one article that falls into the MB&S category. The long-running (founded in 1936) monthly magazine, *Prediction*, caters specifically for writing in this category although many of the regular articles on subjects like Tarot and astrology are pro-duced in-house. Freelance pieces from 800-2,000 words are welcome on Earth Mysteries, power animals and alternative medicine, and often written by well-known authors from the Wiccan community.

To view a cross section of MB&S book titles, go to Ayni Books (**www.ayni-books.com**) and O-Books (**www.o-books.com**), both imprints from the John Hunt publishing stable. Ayni specialises in holistic and alternative health – a subject extremely popular with mainstream women's and health magazines; while O-Books covers the subject of spirituality without any particular religious bias.

Even if you initially feel that there's nothing in mainstream MB&S for you, don't dismiss the genre out of hand. You may discover you're sitting on a wealth of material that could be re-slanted to sit quite comfortably within editorial requirements for non-pagan readers. And remember, some of the best-selling authors in this field are in their 50s and 60s, so it's an exciting new arena for everyone – not just younger writers.

## Exercise

Prepare a list of esoteric subjects that come under your sphere of interest or expertise and separate them into three categories: beginner … intermediate … experienced. For example, we may have a reasonable working knowledge of the Tarot but not consider ourselves an authority on the subject. On the other hand, as an Initiate of a particular Path or Tradition, we should be able to offer a more serious and in-depth approach to belief. Remember that the pagan reader will read your article with a far more critical eye, and that the slightest error will bring forth a torrent of 'letters to the editor', which will ultimately damage your reputation with regard to future submissions.

Select your favourite subject and try to write an opening (i.e. introductory) paragraph for (a) a pagan reader and (b) an MB&S reader. Which did you find easier? And why? Which of the two approaches was the most natural? The results of this exercise should point you in the direction of a compatible readership for the beginner writer, **regardless of your standing within the pagan community.**

> ➤ Remember that all successful writers had to start somewhere.

## Interview: Opportunities For Writers at 6th Books
**Suzanne Ruthven talks to Barbara Ford-Hammond, publisher of 6th Books, which focuses on the fascinating world of the paranormal and parapsychology.**

**SR**: Your guidelines contain a pretty impressive list within parapsychology: investigations, explanations and deliberations on the paranormal, supernatural, explainable or unexplainable. Is there any subject that you are particularly interested in at the moment?

**BFH:** I am pleased to receive all books that fit the imprint but any that teach something new or in different ways are always pleasing. The whole paranormal and parapsychological genre is so fascinating that I am a bit nervous saying one thing... but, there is a lot of interest in anything to do with 'the afterlife'.

**SR:** This is a field that has a more scientific approach to occult subjects and phenomena, but how much experience or background expertise should would-be authors have when approaching you with initial inquiries? Is there room for laypeople on your titles list? And if so, what are the criteria for accepting work from them?

**BFH:** If authors are quoting or reporting then good citing must be used. 6th readers are shrewd and are attracted to particular subject matters as well as to individual authors and would know if someone were feigning expertise. Life experience is as valuable as certificates and some phenomena rely on belief or faith rather than science. We must all respect each other but obey the rule that no harm is done.

**SR:** What type of material do you not want to receive?

**BFH:** I do not like books that are critical of other people or their beliefs. I don't want anything that begins with, 'This will be bigger than Twilight or Harry Potter.' Unless it will! Memoirs can be hard to place unless the author is very well known but readers like a little bit of personal interaction if relevant. The reader must get something for their money and effort of reading: knowledge, new skills, entertainment, emotional experience or a combination.

If you are working on a typescript that you think might be of interest to 6th Books, submit your inquiry in the first instance via the 6th Books website. **www.6th-books.com**

Chapter Two

# Pagan Magazines

There are hundreds of magazines worldwide that will accept freelance material from budding pagan writers. To discover them we need to make a detailed study of the marketplace from the country in which we live. According to Wikipedia, magazines, periodicals, glossies or serials are 'publications generally published on a regular schedule and contain a wide variety of written articles by freelance writers. They are generally financed by advertising, by a purchase price, by pre-paid magazine subscriptions, or all three.'

Pagan magazine publishing is no different, although the revenue generated from advertising is largely dependent on the distribution and quality of the publication. Some of the more esoteric rely solely on subscriptions and these often have a loyal following, supporting the editor with subscriptions and submissions. Others are journals of pagan organisations, although you don't always have to be a member to buy the magazine.

## Developing an Idea

Producing good, marketable ideas in writing is just the same as preparing a vegetable garden and needs the same formula of sowing, fertilising, watering, pruning and, following the harvesting, new and exciting ways of serving. Once the idea begins to germinate, resist the urge to send it off as quickly as possible. Many a good idea has fallen on stony ground by an over-zealous application of enthusiasm. It doesn't matter whether the idea is eventually going to manifest in the shape of a poem or short story, the development stages are going to be the same. Make as many notes as possible and let the idea run around in your mind; play with the idea, tease it but don't make any attempt to write down the first thing that comes into your head.

What you are looking for is the original slant that is going to hook the editor's attention and hold it. Don't forget that most editors have seen it all before and it's not always easy to come up with something original and exciting; as we all know, there's nothing new under the sun, moon and stars – or in creative writing.

**Sowing** the idea is the easy part, but before doing anything with your notes, try looking at it from a different angle or perspective. If the original idea was intended for 20-something females, then try looking at it through the eyes of a child, man or elderly person. Each pair of eyes will see the situation from a different angle – and this applies to all forms of writing.

A good **fertilising** agent is the perusal of where you think the finished piece might appear. The house-style of a magazine will indicate the approach and language acceptable by the editor and put *you* in the position of communicating directly with the readership. In other words: research your intended market so you know exactly who you're writing for. If your idea is for a full-length book then your fertilising techniques need to be even more far reaching. Here you need to take into account what's already in publication and what's about to be published, especially when it comes to non-fiction. See what's available from the local library and ask your local bookseller for any current publisher catalogues,. These are published twice a year and give details of forthcoming titles. Also do on-lines searches. Publishers don't want a repeat of what someone else has written, so the wider your knowledge of the market, the better chance you have of producing something original.

**Watering** your idea with plenty of carefully researched material gives an impression of space and depth even with the most economical use of words, i.e. poetry. Nonfiction, particularly, needs to contain original material that hasn't appeared in print before. Fiction can also score points if the setting is out of the ordinary – even if the storyline is familiar. This is one of the most important stages, since over-writing can drench the piece with superfluous description, while under-writing usually leaves the piece devoid of any features to inspire empathy, sympathy or loathing.

**Pruning** your work is something that shouldn't be rushed, but when in doubt: dig it out. By now your idea will have grown into something quite large and impressive but it's got to be tailor-made for your target market, so start looking for ways to make it slicker and sharper. Don't be tempted to send some long rambling saga when the maximum length for submission is 2,000 words. It may be that you've too much information for a full-length non-fiction book, so look at those odd paragraphs that don't really fit, even if they do contain interesting anecdotes. Take them out and use them for articles to promote the book, especially if you're writing on a specialist subject. If the articles sell, enclose copies with the proposal when it goes off to a publisher. This shows interest on the marketing front. Whatever we write, there is *always* too much detail in the first draft and the mark of the professional is knowing when and what to cut.

**Harvesting** ensures you have several possible outlets in mind. This doesn't mean you're going to send the *identical* piece to each of them – are you? Each publisher/editor has a house-style and so your submission needs to be compatible. We've come back to understanding what editors want, and you can never have too much information in *that* department. Make it your business to find out what's going on in the publishing world because just as much attention needs to be paid to marketing your work as writing it. And finally, when **serving up** your finished piece, don't spoil all this hard work and effort by submitting a poorly presented manuscript.

## Preserving an idea

What happens if your wonderful idea isn't quite ready for working on? Notes ... notes ... and more notes. Keep a notebook by you at all times and jot down anything and everything that comes into your mind. We often find that whenever we have an idea, we'll find information comes our way without looking for it in the form of related items appearing in the media. Keep notes from the TV and radio, cuttings from magazines and newspapers, and bookmark websites. You won't use everything, but a line here or a quote there will help to add depth and credibility to your writing – especially if you are a beginner. The experienced writer learns to recognise these 'extras' and not rely on the same old material over and over again.

Some writers believe that too much market information stifles creativity, but it does pay to know your market. A good idea is all very well, but if you haven't learned how to nurture and develop it, then it may shrivel and die. Ideas are the life-blood of creative writing: this piece started off as a throw away comment about the similarities between writing and growing vegetable marrows!

## Popular Pagan Magazines

By taking a look at a handful of the most popular pagan magazines, we can begin to see the subtle differences between them in style and approach to the wider spectrum of pagan belief. We need to study the editorials, advertising and artwork to gain a useful insight into the mind of the editor.

### Pagan Dawn

*Pagan Dawn* is the quarterly journal of the Pagan Federation that has grown professionally since it began life as *The Wiccan* in 1969. The editor accepts submissions from readers of all pagan paths from full-length pieces of approximately 1,750 words; featured 'tradition' and 'deity' pieces of between 700-800 words; letters and 'fillers' of under 500 words. There is no payment for submissions but *Pagan Dawn* can be obtained by subscription without joining the Pagan Federation. See **www.paganfed.org/pdawn**

## Witchcraft & Wicca

This is an A5-size quarterly journal of Children of Artemis and features articles by many leading names in the pagan community. The content of the magazine is very similar to *Pagan Dawn* in terms of subject matter and keeps things at a basic level for newcomers to the pagan scene. Available by subscription – see www.witchcraft.org

## Pentacle

Edited by Marion Pearce, *Pentacle* is probably the UK's most popular independent pagan magazine and certainly the most approachable. This quarterly magazine caters for pagans of all paths (especially beginners) and the articles feature a wide range of relevant issues such as the environment, sacred sites, herbalism, crafts and history. Go to the website at www.pentaclemagazine.co.uk for more information.

## Prediction

This monthly mainstream publication has been going since 1936 and describes itself as a mind, body and spirit magazine despite the fact that it will feature articles on witchcraft and Wicca. Its guidelines run along the lines of: 'Serving up a delectable menu of spiritual treats, expect to find astrology, divination, lunar phases, yoga, Western, Chinese and Native American horoscopes, meditation, spiritual courses and workshops. We also include shamanism, Wicca and pagan subjects, Tarot, dreams, holistic health, flower remedies, spiritual awakening, kundalini, Ayurveda, eco-news and products, crystals and tantra, and all bound up with a massive dose of LOVE.' Go to the website at **www.predictionmagazine.co.uk** for more information although the magazine is available from most newsagents.

## Kindred Spirit

*Kindred Spirit* is a bi-monthly magazine, first published in 1987, which also describes itself as a mind, body and spirit publication. Each issue 'covers a range of diverse subjects such as spiritual growth, personal development, complementary therapies, travel, health, etc.,' but will accept material on shamanism and Wicca. See **www.kindredspirit.co.uk** for more information.

## Deosil Dance

Edited by Kim Morgan, Deosil Dance describes itself as a 'magazine dedicated to the beliefs and practices of pagan faiths in the 21st century' and welcomes submissions from all pagan writers. Go to **www.deosildance.co.uk** for submission details.

## Brigid's Fire

Brigid's Fire is Ireland's quarterly magazine that covers all aspects of esoteric writing on a serious level. Many of the regular contributors are internationally known pagan authors and although the material used is of general interest, priority is given to writers living in Ireland, or who have Irish roots. See **www.brigidsfiremagazine.com**

## Witches & Pagans

Looking further afield to the USA, *Witches & Pagans* offers regular columns that 'cover a wide variety of practical, down-to-earth topics including spell-casting, devotional practice, solitary (and family) spirituality, pagan ethics and even magical living on a budget; our no-holds-barred reviews tune you into the best in pagan music and literature (and tells you what to avoid!), while our short fiction, poetry, and letters provide plenty of pagan-centric inspiration and entertainment in every 96-page issue.' See **www.witchesandpagans.com/** for more information.

## The Cauldron

This is best described as the 'pagan magazine for grown-ups' and as it says on the website: 'Our readers and writers represent a broad spectrum of belief and practice from beginners to experienced practitioners. Many of our contributors are well-known published authors and over the last thirty-six years ... have included many other leading witches, magicians and occultists. *The Cauldron's* editor, Michael Howard, has written over thirty books on magic, witchcraft, Earth Mysteries and folklore, and has been involved in witchcraft and magical traditions for forty years. The writers in *The Cauldron* therefore offer a wide range of knowledge and experience you will not find in any other magazine.' For more information about this internationally popular magazine go to: **www.the-cauldron.org.uk/**

## What Editors and Publishers Want

One of the most important things that beginners need to learn is the correct way to make submissions to editors and publishers. This is what we mean by 'market research' and it's a good thing to bear in mind that most professional freelance writers *don't write anything* unless they know where they are going to send it. So knowing the market *does* make sense because editors of pagan publications like to feel that the writer has identified their own particular readership.

This means our being completely familiar with the whole pagan marketplace. In other words, *all* the areas where we would like to see our work in print. That is why we need to know **who** publishes who; **why** they might be interested in our work; **what** stance they take in terms of politics, social mores, sex and morals; **where** to look for their barriers or boundaries; and **how** to approach them.

In order to fully understand what editors want to receive, we need to understand what it's like to sit in the editor's chair and for this exercise, I'm wearing the joint hats of the editor of *The New*

*Writer* and commissioning editor of Compass Books, as well as author of over 30 books in the esoteric genre, to try to answer some of those questions. What we must do is step over to the other side of the desk and look at the whole field of creative writing through the editor's eyes. Once we begin to understand what goes onto the 'slush pile' and what gets a second reading, we've taken the first step to becoming a professional writer **from the editor's point of view.**

An editor's job is to fill the magazine with a complementary selection of stories, features, interviews and fillers. A great deal of this material can be generated in-house, but there are still lots of pages to be filled by freelance writers, especially if we're looking at weekly or monthly publications. Unless we've bothered to study a few recent copies of the magazine, however, we will be unaware of what current trends or viewpoints are being reflected in the publication. These social trends are reflected in both fiction and non-fiction – and an editor wants something topical, so the wise writer scans the newspapers – national and local – for ideas that are pertinent to the pagan community, or readers of the mainstream MB&S magazines.

A considerable amount of material that arrives on the editor's desk is:

- already out of date;
- has obviously been regurgitated several times over;
- a clone of what has been running before;
- has not been written specifically for that target readership;
- does not reflect the house-style of the magazine;
- is well-written but not sparky enough to retain the reader's interest.

And all of these will be instantly rejected ...

This is where we need to develop lateral thinking. We might think our idea is brilliant and exciting but nine times out of ten, we've only written from the first layer of thought that's come into our mind. And how many writers have thought, 'They've nicked my story!' when they've seen something almost identical in print? This is because a large number of other people have been influenced by the same stimuli that started their own creative juices flowing – a modern example of the Collective Unconscious!

As I explained in *LifeWrites*, the key to any editor's or publisher's heart is originality. Not necessarily a new departure in style or genre, but a refreshing and original *approach* to a popular theme. The writer who gets their work accepted has managed to spark the editor's interest because that particular piece stands out from the rest on a dull, wet Monday morning. And the first question we need to ask ourselves is: *why* did it stand out from the rest? What was so special about that particular piece of writing? What made the editor choose to publish it over all the other hundreds of typescripts arriving in the office during that month?

- It may have been brilliantly written – but so are dozens of others.
- It was probably topical – but so are dozens of others.
- It may have met the criteria of every point in the contributor's guidelines – but so did dozens of others.

The answer is that the writer's approach to that common or popular theme was so fresh and appealing that it was almost as if the editor was reading about the subject for the first time. In other words: originality. But where do those original thoughts come from and how do we access them? Although I've gone into the subject in some detail in *LifeWrites*, here are ten points to ponder that might help on a more subliminal level:

- There are more ideas locked away in our unconscious minds than we could ever write about in a whole lifetime, but they can influence our creative writing.

- There is a story, article or poem behind everything we encounter during our daily routine in both the inner and outer worlds if we have the courage to experiment and explore.
- No matter how mundane and/or familiar a scene, there are countless different angles from which to view it.
- We are unique: no one can access the same experiences and memories, which means we have the ability to generate unique responses to situations.
- Creative energy fuels creativity, so immerse yourself in images and stimulating art forms to give fresh ideas and ignite the creative flame.
- Encourage the flow of creative energy from your unconscious mind through visualisation, meditation and relaxation.
- Use your imagination when exploring other artistic mediums such as painting, sculpture, music, etc., because creativity is a state of mind.
- Give your imagination free rein and open up your unconscious mind to the creative possibilities around you; if necessary do the opposite of what is considered the norm.
- By connecting to our subconscious minds we can explore the wealth of universal memories of myth, fantasy, and symbolism – we must use our ability to travel to this hidden world.
- Certain images or symbols open the door to the collective subconscious: try working with these mind pictures to stimulate your creativity no matter how ridiculous they seem at the beginning.

This is why the writer should have this motto taped to the front of their computer: **Throw away the first idea.** Never, never write anything from the first thought that comes into your head. Work at it; worry at it; change it; reverse it, but whatever you do, don't use it – because hundreds of people will have already done the same. Original thought needs to be honed and perfected like any other art form and to be a successful magazine contributor, whether of fact or fiction, we also need to build up a rapport with the editor, so that they know *we* know our stuff. That we are familiar with the editorial content of the magazine and can produce material that slots in comfortably with anything written in-house. We know what's been published in the last year and do not make submissions that are just a repeat of material included three months earlier.

## The Editor's Desk

So what happens to your typescript or proposal when it lands on an editor's desk? In mainstream publishing an unsolicited short story or article by an unknown writer is given approximately **one minute** of the editor's time, or as long as it takes to speed-read the first page. If the editor's attention hasn't been grabbed by those opening paragraphs, then the piece *will* automatically be rejected. This is why it is so essential to ensure that you create a good, snappy opening that makes the editor want to read on. Pagan editors are a little more generous with their time, but the bigger the 'glossy' the more like mainstream editors they will be.

As far as articles, features and interviews are concerned, make an initial enquiry outlining the main points of the article and your reason or experience of pagan/magical practice that allows you to write it. A large number of freelance writers will offer several articles on related topics in order to demonstrate their grasp of the subject and as a showcase for their diverse talents. Initial enquiries can be made via e-mail but unless specifically requested to do so, do not submit the full article by this medium – keep to the double-spaced typescript.

Even if an editor has rejected your work in the past, it still pays to keep an eye on what's going on at that publisher's office.

The average lifespan of an MB&S editor is around two years and then they move on to another magazine. The magazine market is highly competitive and so the in-coming editor will make lots of changes in order to boost sales, or attract a different readership. The editor's job depends on their ability to maintain the magazine's position in the ratings and if they get it wrong, the outcome is yet another change of editor. Generally speaking, however, the editors of pagan publications tend to own the magazine and have been at the helm since the Great Deluge!

My advice to writers is the same as a commissioning editor writing in *The Author:* **look at your work through the eyes of an editor or publisher: start from the book or magazine's point of sale.** Think about who will read it and get to know your market. Think of the key features that distinguish your writing from others who aspire to the same markets. Let your submission be written in a way that a busy commissioning editor will be gripped by what you have on offer.

This is not a matter of dumbing down, trivialising the writing or stifling the creative urge; it is simply the acceptance that at the end of the day publishing is just another consumer outlet. This is not to say that you shouldn't write in your own style or voice, but a professional attitude to contemporary pagan publishing is also an awareness that the successful writer will also have one eye on the *commercial* aspects of the book and magazine market in the MB&S genre, rather than focussing their attention solely on the non-paying pagan markets.

## Exercise

Earlier in this chapter we discussed developing an idea that has a degree of originality in its approach. Now we need to pay attention to selling our idea and this means making sure that the submission letter also has something to catch an editor's eye. We've done our market research; we've studied back issues of the magazine so the next step is to send a carefully constructed proposal for two or three separate articles that should appeal to the editor. Give a two or three sentence description for each idea that conveys the feel of the finished article.

Of course, the longer the period of research, the more familiar you will be with the type of material the editor likes and, even more important, the subjects which have already been covered in recent issues. Quite a lot of submissions are rejected purely and simply because the subject matter is too similar to that recently published, or already accepted and/or commissioned. By obtaining *regular* copies of the magazines you would like to write for, you will be aware of:

- what the editor likes;
- and dislikes;
- what's been run before;
- whether a different approach could make interesting reading;
- questions that are regularly asked;
- answers that don't satisfy;
- a need for good fillers;
- new books under discussion;
- recommended old favourites;
- interesting subjects for 'coffee break' moments.

Your proposal letter should state clearly and succinctly what connection you have with the subject and why you are qualified to write the pieces on offer. Give an indication of the length of each piece so the editor knows what to expect and whether it's in accordance with their own guidelines. Don't complete the piece until the editor emails to say they would like to see the finished article. Since every magazine's requirements are different, it would need revamping, unless it had been written with that particular publication in mind. And remember, the acceptance of an idea in principle isn't a commission. The idea might be fantastic, but if the finished article doesn't come up to scratch then it will be rejected.

Never submit anything with the words, 'This article is highly suitable for your publication'. Experience shows that someone who's never seen the magazine will have written this. The approach is usually incompatible with the magazine's guidelines even if there aren't any hard and fast rules about house-style. This type of letter often refers to the editor by their first name, and so there is a frantic game of mental scrabble, trying to work out who the hell's sent it, and thinking: 'Am I supposed to know them? Have I asked for this submission?' Keep things business-like until you've established regular contact and then be guided by the response you receive.

> First impressions *do* count – they can quickly tell an editor whether they want to work with you, or not.

## Interview: Opportunities for Writers at *Pentacle*

**Suzanne Ruthven talks to Marion Pearce, author and editor of the UK's most popular independent pagan magazine, *Pentacle*. The current quarterly readership is around 15,000, with shops and stockists totalling more than 200 outlets.**

**SR:** *Pentacle* is known for its accessibility for newcomers to the pagan community, but how do you manage to constantly maintain such a welcoming approach towards your readership?

**MP:** I firmly believe that the independent pagan publications, and *Pentacle* in particular, should be accessible to pagans of all paths and of all levels of knowledge. There should be something for everyone and it is very important that those new to paganism should have access to information that is relevant to them. Paganism is one of the fastest growing religions in the UK and many people are now turning to it for its practical assistance in modern life.

**SR:** You include a wide selection of topics for pagans of all

Paths, including the environment, sacred sites, herbalism, crafts and history. What advice would you give to those wanting to write for the magazine?

**MP:** As to future contributors, I like to appeal to those who have an interest in topics suitable for the readership. My writers are people with knowledge. They might not have degrees or qualifications, but are knowledgeable in their own particular field; it is this knowledge that I am seeking. I have always been very impressed with the high level of expertise in both readership and contributors. If you are passionate about a subject, it is likely that others will be too. I welcome new writers: it is an important part of *Pentacle*.

**SR:** You use a selection of interesting and controversial letters, together with poetry, reviews, environmental news and events. Is this a good way for new writers to break into print with you?

**MP:** This is an excellent way to start your writing career. I have watched many pagans start with writing letters and news items; then, as confidence grows, through to writing excellent articles. There is a wealth of hidden talent in the pagan community just waiting to be found.

**SR:** As a non-profit making venture, *Pentacle* doesn't pay for contributions but still includes articles by many famous pagan authors. As an author yourself, do you think the magazine is an ideal place for new writers to showcase their work?

**MP:** *Pentacle* is a work of love – a community magazine and completely non-profit making. The cover price just pays for the printing and postage costs. I started my writing career by writing for pagan magazines. They gave me a wonderful base to hone my skills. I went on to write books for the pagan market and now have five books published by three different pagan publishing houses.

**SR:** Is there any type of material you don't want to receive?

**MP:** *Pentacle* does not publish fiction.

**If you feel you have a contribution that would be suitable**

for *Pentacle* magazine, e-mail editor@pentaclemagazine.co.uk
Articles should not exceed 2,000 words, although the content is
more important than length. www.pentaclemagazine.co.uk

Chapter Three

# Pagan Book Publishers

Begin by submitting short articles to the different quarterly pagan magazines and the monthly MB&S publications, to gauge the editor appeal of your subject and writing style. If you have work accepted, *then* you can begin to look at book publishers who specialise in pagan material – check out the submission guidelines to see if your idea fits their titles list and then send an inquiry in the first instance.

On a much broader scale, similar rules to magazine submissions also apply if you are thinking of submitting a proposal for a full-length book to a publisher. In a recent issue of *The Author*, the quarterly journal of the Society of Authors, a commissioning editor was unexpectedly quite frank about the fact that if a proposed title is unlikely to contribute significantly to the following year's turnover, the publishing house is unlikely to take it, no matter how much they happen to like the book and/or the author.

Start by studying the writing style of popular authors and try to learn from their individual techniques – a good cross section of pagan book titles in print can be viewed at John Hunt Publishing at the following imprints: Moon Books (witchcraft, pagan and shamanic), 6th Books (paranormal and parapsychology), Axis Mundi (esoteric and magical), Dodona (divination); or Capall Bann Publishing (general pagan subjects) and Llewellyn Worldwide (all esoteric subjects).

## Getting a Foot In The Door

When the commissioning editor at the publishing house receives a submission, it can go in one of two directions. Send a full typescript, with a covering letter addressed to 'Dear Sir or Madam' or with a wrong name on it and it *will* land up on the 'slush pile' where it can sit for months, until the youngest (and most resentful) reader is told to sift through the pile and get rid of as many as they can.

To be quite frank, submitting unsolicited full typescripts just wastes everyone's time and the only ones to benefit are the Post Office and the telephone companies, if you persist in chasing it. Hopefully, all of us know that the correct way to submit to a publisher is by sending a synopsis and two sample chapters, having first telephoned the company to check on the name of the correct editor. Also check whether they accept submissions by email – **and never, never deviate from this process unless you are told to do otherwise.**

Let us imagine for a moment that a commissioning editor has received your synopsis and sample chapters. For good form, you have enclosed a covering letter/email containing a brief biography and information relating to any serious published work. By 'serious' I mean published work that relates to the subject covered in your proposed book. There is little point in including details of an occasional piece accepted by the editor of the parish magazine when the subject matter of your book is quantum physics. Make sure that what you include *is* relevant. On the other hand, if you are a regular contributor or columnist for an unrelated publication, this *is* worth a mention, because it shows that you are a disciplined writer and can work to deadlines. And let's face it, we need all the help we can get.

Let's go back to the commissioning editor writing in *The Author:* visualise her about to present your typescript to the publishing committee. Around the table are seated the editorial directors, sales and marketing people and the accountants. If your typescript has been sent to one of the publishing giants, then there won't be just colleagues from her own imprint, there will be editors from other imprints as well, all clutching the proposals they wish to put before the committee that day. In-house the competition is fierce and, according to a literary agent of my acquaintance, it is pointless sending a proposal to different imprints within the same company, as the same publishing committee considers them all.

Now we come to the important bit. The commissioning editor holding your proposal has just **five minutes** to explain what your book is about; why it will be a success; to justify the sales figures; *and* wax convincingly about the author's value to the list. According to our inside information, for an editor to take a book to committee and have it rejected is an acute embarrassment and shows lack of judgement. Therefore in assessing your proposals, she is going to ask herself:

- Can I get this past the committee?
- Can I sell the idea in five minutes?
- Can I fire the committee's enthusiasm?
- Can I convince them it will be a profitable venture?

If the answer to any of those question is 'no' the proposal *will* be rejected at the reading stage and I quote:

To the author I would say this: 'If you can sell me the idea for your book in five minutes, I'll be able to sell it to a publishing committee in the same time span, and so will the rep in the book shop, or selling to buyers from the major book chains, for whom this is just one of twenty titles. If you cannot do this, or insist that I have to read the whole typescript to appreciate its significance, your book stands little chance.'

For non-fiction titles, all I need is a brief summary of what the book is about, an indication of its intended readership, the proposed length and how it compares with similar titles already published. I also need to know what the author has already published, why he or she is particularly keen or qualified to write this book and when – if commissioned – it could be delivered. If the book looks a possible one for my list,

I may then ask for a chapter-by-chapter summary of contents and a sample to show style. That is quite enough; with proposals, more generally means worse.

Perhaps here we should say a word about simultaneous submissions. We are told that a proposal should only be sent to one publishing house at a time. Bearing in mind that it can take anything up to six months to get a response, under this ruling it means that the author can only submit the proposal twice a year! My view is that having worked out which publishing houses are likely to be interested in a book, these should be approached in batches of two or three. Some will respond quickly, but if we haven't heard within six weeks, send off another batch. If those dragging their heels miss out, that's not our problem.

If a publisher asks to see the complete typescript, don't send to any other publisher until you have a 'yes' or 'no'. Give them three months and if you still don't get a reply, start sending out from where you left off, but don't withdraw the typescript from those who already have it. Keep *all* of your options open. When I was tutoring a workshop at Cheltenham Literary Festival, one participant who worked as a commissioning editor for a large publishing house violently disagreed with my recommendations that the would-be author should tout themselves around in this manner. She said it was unethical. When pressed, however, she finally had to admit that *she* couldn't get a definite 'yes' or 'no' on a book in under three months.

I rest my case...

## Sympathetic Pagan Book Publishers

A large number of mainstream publishers now have a MB&S imprint, and even those who have no connection to either pagan or 'alternative' beliefs may offer opportunities for our writing. We need to become a sleuth to track down those more elusive outlets. For example, **Country Books (www.countrybooks.biz)**

publishes the 'Ghost walks of Britain' series, while **Shire Books** (**www.shirebooks.co.uk**) has a 'History, heritage and nostalgia' series that includes folklore, rural history and bygones and which might offer opportunities in another genre to pagan writers.

Mainstream publisher, **Robert Hale** (**www.halebooks.com**) has a MB&S imprint that *does* include titles by Patricia Crowther, Doreen Valiente, Stewart and Janet Farrar, and Rae Beth, and an assortment of other titles that are geared more towards paganism and Wicca. **The History Press** (**www.thehistorypress.co.uk**) publishes more academic books, but has titles in its 'Local history' series that include folk-tales, hauntings and the paranormal.

If you feel more comfortable with sympathetic 'spiritual publishers', you can turn to the different imprints of **John Hunt** (**www.johnhuntpublishing.com**) who caters for *all* aspects of spirituality, paganism and environmental subjects – both mainstream and alternative:

- Firstly, **6<sup>th</sup> Books** specialises in the paranormal and parapsychology – i.e. investigations, explanations and deliberations on the paranormal, supernatural, explainable or unexplainable. '6th seeks to give answers while nourishing the soul: whether making use of the scientific model or anecdotal and fun, but always beautifully written. Titles cover everything included within parapsychology: how to, lifestyles, alternative medicine, beliefs, myths, theories and memoir.'

AXIS MUNDI
BOOKS

- The editor of **Axis Mundi** welcomes submissions for all esoteric subjects. 'Axis Mundi Books provide the most revealing and coherent explorations and investigations of the world of hidden or forbidden knowledge. Take a fascinating journey into the realm of esoteric mysteries; high magic (non-pagan); mysticism; mystical worlds; angels; aliens; cosmology; alchemy and alternative views of mainstream religion.'

- **Dodona Books** specialises in divination. 'The oracle was an early form of divination, and divination has existed perhaps as long as humankind itself. We use divination to foresee future possibilities, to answer questions about our lives, to explain the unexplainable, for revealing hidden dynamics in ourselves and others; for personal growth and to guide us onto the right pathway through life. Dodona Books offers a broad spectrum of divination systems to suit everyone.'

MOON
BOOKS

- The **Moon Books** imprint covers the area of witchcraft, paganism and shamanism and forces us to ask ourselves … 'What is paganism? A religion, a spirituality, an alternative belief system, nature worship? You can find support for all these definitions (and many more) in dictionaries, encyclopaedias, and textbooks of religion, but subscribe to any one and the truth will evade you. Above all paganism is a creative pursuit, an encounter with reality, an exploration of meaning and an expression of the soul. Druids, Heathens, Wiccans and others, all contribute their insights and literary riches to the pagan tradition ...'

Because there are several overlapping spheres of interest between the imprints, the good thing with John Hunt Publishing is that if your submission doesn't quite suit a particular imprint, one editor will recommend you to try another editor within the group.

**Capall Bann** (www.capallbann.co.uk) is a family-owned and run company that has been publishing pagan titles since 1993, and 'operated by people with real experience in the topics we publish', which include British pagan traditions, folklore, animals, alternative healing, environmental, Celtic lore and MB&S titles.

At the opposite end of the scale we have **Llewellyn Worldwide** (www.llewellyn.com) the 'giant' of esoteric publishing that includes all aspects of alternative health, tantra, metaphysics, magic, witchcraft, shamanism, organic gardening, women's spirituality and parapsychology. It will also consider fiction with an authentic magical or metaphysical theme.

There's a lot of hard work and sleuthing skills involved in tracking down a suitable publisher for a full-length book and in this area of writing, non-fiction will stand more chance of acceptance than a novel. For beginners, my suggestion would be put the novel away until you have some street-cred with the publisher on the strength of good published articles. Also take note of the more specialist publishers of current esoteric titles on your own bookshelves, as well as those in bookshops and listed in magazines, as these are often missing from the writers' handbooks.

## The Proposal

It's often said that it's harder to write a proposal than it is to write a complete book. This is because the proposal must encapsulate an entire 'story' in order for a publisher to judge whether they wish to see the full typescript. Nevertheless, a well-written synopsis, together with the first three chapters of your novel or non-fiction book will tell them all they need to know about your writing ability. Check the writers' guidelines to see if the publisher requires the completed typescript before sending your proposal, as some will not consider a new author unless the finished, final draft is available.

### What you'll need

- A clear idea about what your book is about and who's going to read it.
- Generally speaking, a synopsis should be no longer than an A4 page – single spacing = approx 500 words.
- Only introduce the principal characters and restrict yourself to a thumbnail sketch of each in one sentence per person. Even if the narrative is character driven, a publisher or agent is going to be more interested in the plot.
- Ask yourself: what is my story about? Now retell the story as if you were answering the question asked over dinner – any more than 500 words and your listener's eyes would begin to glaze over with boredom.
- Don't write the synopsis in a chapter-by-chapter style – tell the story as a piece of well crafted mini-fiction.
- And yes … publishers/agents DO want to know how the story ends! Don't make the mistake of thinking that if they

want to know how it ends they will send for the complete typescript. It doesn't work like that.

- Make sure you include important moments of intense highs and lows, but avoid drawn out descriptions of who's doing what to whom.
- Make an opening statement about when and where the story is set. This immediately identifies the period/setting in the reader's mind.
- For a non-fiction book the rules are still the same because you are still telling a story but without characters. Give the reason for writing a new book about the subject, and why you think it will have reader appeal. Also give a hint of any new or original information you have obtained that adds a spark to the subject and justifies a publisher adding the book to his lists.
- A proposal for non-fiction can be submitted as a chapter-by-chapter breakdown, because the publisher can immediately see from the chapters how the book will progress. Opening sample chapters will give an example of your writing.
- Put the finished proposal away in a drawer for a few days before sending it off. Sometimes we can produce something better if we allow our ideas to simmer.

## Conclusion

The importance of a good proposal cannot be stressed strongly enough. Avoid leaving the writing of it until the last minute or you'll look upon it as a job to be got out of the way without too much thought. A rejection or acceptance may hinge on how much effort you've put into writing it. Study the blurb on the cover of recently published books to see how the publisher has encapsulated the content, in order to grab the browser's interest in just a few words. A long, rambling proposal can mean instant rejection of your book

> Opportunity only knocks once – so impress the publisher right from the start

## Exercise

To get a clear idea in your own mind of what you are aiming for in a full-length book, complete the following questionnaire for your own benefit. By clearly defining your target market, you will have a constant reminder of whom you are writing for in terms of age, interest and ability.

- Describe your target market/genre where you think your finished typescript will be aimed.
- Describe your target readership in terms of who you think will enjoy your book.
- Which publishers have a similar approach on their titles list?
- Prepare a 'blurb' in no more than 150 words to show the outline of the subject.

This simple exercise enables us to focus on **exactly who we are writing for** and, having this picture of our readers in our mind's eye, we find it easier to pitch our proposal to the right publisher with a greater degree of confidence.

## Interview: Opportunities for Writers at Axis Mundi

**Suzanne Ruthven talks to Krystina Kellingley about the opportunities with Axis Mundi Books for writers with an interest in esoteric subjects.**

**SR:** Your titles list reveals a fascinating blend of topics from different paths and traditions from around the world. Are we looking at the areas of the occult sciences that aren't necessarily thought of as 'pagan'?

**KK:** Moon Books is our imprint dealing with all things pagan, so yes, pretty much anything outside that would come to Axis

Mundi. There is sometimes a slight cross over and it's decided that a book might be better in another imprint – but if that happens we'll move it to the correct imprint unless the author specifically wants their manuscript to stay where it was submitted.

**SR:** Do prospective authors need to be experienced practitioners of their particular discipline?

**KK:** With our non-fiction, I think it would be virtually impossible to write something informative, fresh or helpful to the reader on a topic you have no knowledge of and no interest in. Many of the subjects Axis Mundi covers require a deep knowledge and personal experience. We do publish some fiction and although if you had no knowledge at all of the subject you had based your story on you would need to do your research, you wouldn't need to be an expert.

**SR:** Are there any particular subjects you'd like to include on your forthcoming titles list?

**KK:** I'd quite like to see some factual evidence of past lives or continuing existence after death. I don't mean haunting as such or ghosts – something on a deeper, spiritual level.

**SR:** Is there any type of material you don't want to receive?

**KK:** We'll look at any type of esoteric subject material but we are an ethical company so whatever we decide to publish would have to be bound by that consideration.

**SR:** Have you any additional words of advice for anyone who sees themselves as a potential Axis Mundi author?

**KK:** If you feel you have something of interest to show to the world; that your particular knowledge or experience would be beneficial, inspirational or offer new insight to others then just go for it. Sit down and start to write. If you find yourself enjoying the laying down of your ideas onto a page and that the words keep flowing then keep going, you have something to share and we might be the right publisher to help you do that. **www.axismundi-books.com**

Chapter Four

# The On-Line Pagan Community

The widest pagan outlet is, of course, the Internet with all its attendant blogs, websites, twitters, Facebook pages and e-books. Unfortunately, as the old saying goes: *'On the Internet nobody knows you're a cat!'* and nobody knows whether anyone is a well-read amateur, or an experienced magical practitioner! For obvious reasons, few people use their 'real' names and more often than not, it is necessary to 'sign up' to gain access to the inner sanctum of the site without actually knowing who the contact may be.

Trial and error is the order of the day and bearing in mind the Old Craft adage of 'Trust None!' – it is necessary to trawl through the multitude of pagan listings until you find one that feels right for you. For example, I have three that I contribute to on a regular basis, which have been around for a long time ...

### Moon Books Facebook and Blog

There's a lot of social networking goes on via this blog and it's useful for keeping up to date on what's going on with those who have an interest in writing for the pagan community. Here I have a Q&A input that stems from the questions I'm regularly asked at workshops and by students on the Arcanum foundation course.

See the Interview at the end of the chapter.

### Witches & Pagans

Pagan Square is the blog of the American-based magazine, *Witches & Pagans* edited by Anne Newkirk Niven of BBI Media News, who also produces *Crone* and *SageWoman* magazines. This is a very broad-based approach to all matters pagan and I have my own 'Root & Branch' blog for traditional British Old Craft, just as other contributors cover Heathen and Northern, Celtic, native and Aboriginal paths, earth wisdom and all aspects of pagan culture. Separate guidelines are available upon request for poetry, reviews, interviews, and debate essays – see **www.witch esandpagans.com** and link to the blogs and Facebook pages.

## Witch Vox or Witches Voice

Possibly one of the best known pagan community websites that describes itself as being a 'proactive educational network providing news, educational services and resources for and about pagans, Heathens, witches and Wiccans.' Here we can find almost any kind of contact anywhere in the world and be able to post articles for the pagan community to read; the site can direct us to thousands of other pagan websites and list some 64 categories pertinent to pagan interest – both magical and social – see **www.witchvox.com** and link to the Facebook page. In the 'authors and publishers' section, I list all my current titles and publicise any new books in advance of the publication date.

There are, of course, websites run by respected members of the pagan community such as **www.callaighe.com** the official website of Janet Farrar and Gavin Bone, and those of other established pagan authors, which will often point in the direction of other reputable sites. Needless to say, however, there are literally thousands of websites, blogs and Facebook pages from around the globe that encourage submissions from pagan writers. Let the writer beware, however, as there are no guarantees as to the magical standing of the content, or of those operating the websites.

Try a Google search for 'pagan websites' and there are around 5,920,000 to choose from – while 'best pagan websites' produced 20,700,000 on offer. Type in 'pagan links' and we come up with a further 22,900,000; with 'wiccan websites' producing 9,750,000 searches and 'witches websites' a further 3,320,000!

## By Rule of Thumb

If you wish to contribute material to a pagan blog or access a pagan Facebook page, it will be necessary to register first, although you can usually get an idea of the depth and length of the writing the organisers will accept, without having to log in. Bear in mind that pagan organisations have been the target of virulent abuse in the past, and for security reasons, very few pagan 'personalities' will operate under their true identities – old habits die hard.

And just because these on-line contributions are instant postings, it doesn't mean that our approach should be any the less professional when it comes to writing or accuracy. Compose your article as a text file, just as you would for a magazine submission, and hone it until you are completely satisfied that it is the best you can produce. Make sure that you quote all your sources and give a final spell-check before cut and pasting it onto the blog.

Most professional writers in any genre would tell you that a large percentage of material posted on the web wouldn't pass muster by a magazine editor or publisher. Magically speaking, not only are there glaring inaccuracies in the content (which reveals the inexperience of the poster), but there are also pages of what Michael Howard of *The Cauldron* refers to as 'vanilla-lite paganism', which does not find favour with those of the more traditional Paths.

Study each website as diligently as you would a magazine or publisher's back list, and discover for yourself the level of experience the site is catering for. By rule of thumb, material generally falls into three categories: beginner, intermediate and experienced – with beginners writing for beginners; those at an intermediary stage aiming at those at a similar level on the Path, while the more highly experienced often write for the beginners and give nothing away!

## Fact and Fakelore

Perhaps we are now in a better position to define what we mean by 'paganism' from a **publishing perspective** rather than a spiritual standpoint. Although in publishers' catalogues every-thing is often lumped together under the collective banner of mind, body and spirit, a large number of the reading public embrace the MB&S ethos without having the slightest leanings towards the magical or mystical. Similarly, many of those who refer to themselves as 'pagan' are completely divorced from the *practical* concept of traditional witchcraft and shamanism.

As David V Barrett observes in *The New Believers*, there is also a considerable crossover between the various esoteric movements and neo-paganism.

> For example, although the esoteric movements are usually Eastern-based or Judaeo-Christian in origin, some of them are closer to Goddess-worship, which is essentially pagan. Similarly, although the neo-pagan movements are mainly based on Celtic, Norse or Native American traditions, many also use Tarot, and some Kabbala, which are essentially esoteric ... In addition to the specific groups [or traditions], there are millions of individual people who belong to no movement, but who have some interest in what are loosely called 'New Age' ideas.

As Barrett goes on to explain, a glance at the MB&S shelves in any general bookshop, or at the contents of a specialist esoteric bookshop, will reveal books on every related subject. For the purists of a particular path or tradition, however, the search for 'advanced' reading material is more difficult, simply because books catering for basic or superficial interests are more financially viable than what might be described as 'advanced instruction'.

It is often difficult to judge our own level of working and the way we represent our esoteric experience in terms of a **publishable mainstream typescript**. The language differs between beginner and intermediary levels, although there are some subjects that often defy us to write about at an elementary level.

Take, for example, a book I wrote some years ago called *The Hollow Tree*, an elementary guide to the Qabalah and Tarot (ignotus press), which attempted to introduce the subject with the minimum amount of confusion. Although linking both systems together for the purpose of the 'magical' version, it was important to convey that the origins and antecedents of both were completely unrelated, and had undergone multiple translations, adaptations, additions and changes across the centuries. The version familiar to 21st century occultists is that expanded and revised in the 19th and 20th centuries when it metamorphosed into a mystical 'snakes and ladders'. Whichever way we look at it, the subject is not one that easily lends itself to elementary guides, and although I remain satisfied with the result, it is almost impossible to convey even the basics without using esoteric language, which is incomprehensible to a beginner.

Conversely, we can take the subject of domestic folk-medicine – *Memory, Wisdom and Healing: The History of Domestic Plant Medicine* by Gabrielle Hatfield (Sutton), that is written as a 'study of the folklore of modern Britain as well as a fascinating piece of social history' without any designs on an 'alternative' readership and find that it translates into both pagan and the MB&S markets at all levels.

What we must also accept is that while a large amount of pagan belief is eclectic – it also rejects what it doesn't like or find acceptable. For example, when submitting the proposal for *By Spellbook & Candle: Cursing, Hexing, Bottling & Binding*, one of the

American readers, Anne Newkirk Niven, made the observation: 'Here in the US virtually no modern neo-pagan will admit to cursing, and the topic is basically taboo. For example, any review in my magazine, *Witches & Pagans*, would have to include pretty heavy disclaimers about the ethics of cursing.' While the UK reaction from Michael Howard of *The Cauldron* commented: 'It is refreshing in these days of vanilla-lite witchcraft that someone actually acknowledges that modern witches can and do curse.' Nimue Brown of The Druid Network felt that: 'It's good to see someone having the courage to take on this subject. Many writers on the subject of witchcraft prefer to say 'We don't go there' and 'Just don't' and leave it at that.'

So, we must also be mindful of the parameters set by publishers and editors for the benefit of their readership and take care that our writing does not infringe the contributors' guidelines. We may not always agree with what we see as 'dumbing down' or trivialising a belief, but the power of our writing may persuade others to at least consider a different viewpoint for a moment.

➤ This is what it means to be a 'professional writer'.

## Interview: Opportunities for Writers at Moon Books

**Suzanne Ruthven talks to Trevor Greenfield about the rapidly growing popularity of Moon Books for non-fiction and fiction and the strong support the publishing imprint has with the on-line pagan community.**

**SR:** You have an impressive collection of titles, most of them relating to paganism, witchcraft, Wicca, Druidry, Norse and shamanism ... is it difficult to discover new voices in these areas?

**TG:** No, to be honest it hasn't proved that difficult. We have developed a strong on-line presence and I think that has helped new writers to find us. That, and the fact that we assess and make decisions on proposals in days rather than the more traditional publishers that still take months to decide, encourages submissions.

**SR:** It's often been said that if you were to ask 100 witches to define their beliefs, you would have a 100 different answers. Do you have any particular bias for one particular system or another?

**TG:** No, we have no preference. We have published a number of titles on Traditional Witchcraft but that's simply because they are what has come in. We have recently started a new series called Pagan Portals which is designed for pagans to write about their particular skills, interests or knowledge so that should hopefully encourage diversity in the submissions we receive.

**SR:** Have you any additional advice for potential Moon Books authors – and in particular, what sort of material would be instantly rejected?

**TG:** My advice would be submit! We have a friendly, informal and very fast submission process. You'll know within a week or so what our decision is and either way our feedback will include reader reports that will hopefully be of use to the author regardless of our decision. I don't usually instantly reject anything but if I do it's when the submission takes the form of an overly romanticised potted author bio with limited detail on the actual book. Keep the info tight and relevant. It might, for example, be of familial interest that the author has been a witch for forty years and can recall magical holidays spent at her grandmother's cottage where she passed on her knowledge of herbal medicine, but sadly it doesn't follow that you are empowered to write a good book.

**SR:** I see that you've recently introduced Pagan Moon Fiction that offers the opportunity for pagan fiction writers. This is an important addition but not one I would have thought financially viable since mainstream fiction is extremely difficult to sell, never mind fiction from a 'niche' market. So how are you going to make it work?

**TG:** Since starting Moon Books I've continually been asked if we publish pagan fiction. I've hated having to say 'no' to so many writers so we've developed a scheme that allows fiction writers to publish with us. Moon Books now publishes fiction with the support of an author subsidy to help cover production costs.

**SR:** So what we are talking about is 'subsidy publishing' whereby the author contributes to the production costs but has access to all the editing, production and marketing facilities of the publisher. How do you maintain the quality of the writing?

**TG:** From Moon Books' perspective the requirement for quality remains paramount. We will read the text and only accept it if we consider the manuscript is worthy of publication and it fits the list, that is, in our case, if we feel confident and comfortable with it as a Moon Book.

If you are writing a book on any of the different pagan disciplines and think it may be of interest to Moon Books, submit your inquiry via the website in the first instance **www.moon-books.net**

# Chapter Five

# A Pagan Reference Library

Every writer needs a good reference library that reflects the subject matter about which they write – it means instant access to (often out of print) information, reminders of what other authors have written, and differing (often opposing) viewpoints. All of which is grist to the writer's mill. If, like me, books are an addiction, then it becomes necessary every few years to weed out those that are no longer useful or relevant but we also need to be mindful about what we throw away. Some old books, once discarded, cannot be replaced and somewhere along the line, we *will* regret parting with them.

Some of the following will be familiar reading, while others will offer different insights to certain esoteric subjects. Needless to say, your choice will not be the same as mine, and will probably differ considerably from another writer, but generally speaking, a pagan writer's reference library should consist of at least one serious title in the following categories:

## Astronomy – Astrology

Two completely separate disciplines but both are essential reference books for the pagan writer – one is a science and the other an art. **Astronomy** is the study of the celestial bodies and heavens from all scientific aspects, although the origin of the study of the stars dates back to ancient Egypt, when it was an integral part of the pre-dynastic religion. In fact, all the early astronomer-priesthoods viewed the heavens in religious terms because the sky was believed to be the home of the gods; they studied all celestial activity, maintained records, compiled calendars, and acted as keepers of the myths and legends of the sky-gods.

Although the Greeks accredited the Egyptians with recognising the movement of the stars and the creation of the earliest 'star-clocks', most of the information that has filtered through from ancient times is Greek and Roman in origin – even the great Dendera zodiac. The Greek and Babylonian influences of the Ptolemaic period (305-30AD) introduced the 'zodiac' as we know it today (see **Zodiac**). Because the astronomer Ptolemy had the same name as the Graeco-Egyptian pharaohs, and lived in Alexandria, it is understandable that many, incorrectly, assume him to be Egyptian. It was Ptolemy, however, who gathered together the material for his great astronomical treatise, usually known under its Arabic title of *Almagest*, published around 150AD in 13 books.

The *Almagest* begins with a description of the nature of the universe and provides a systematic treatment of the whole of mathematical astronomy. In Books 7 and 8, Ptolemy discusses the question of 'fixed' stars and the phenomenon of precession, which he demonstrates by showing that there had been systematic changes in the declinations of certain stars. He also gives a star catalogue, which consists of 1,022 stars arranged under 48 constellations. In *The Amateur Astronomer*, Sir Patrick Moore lists 39 of those known to Ptolemy and identifiable today. Some of these constellations are no longer visible, while others can no longer be seen with the naked eye.

In contemporary magic, however, it is still essential to have a rudimentary grasp of what we see in the night sky from both the northern and southern hemisphere, even if it's only a reference to the mythology represented by the constellations and planets. The best references being *The Box of Stars* by Catherine Tennant, who uses copies of the original *Urania's Mirror* published in London c1825, as an original and easy way to get to know the heavens; and the more scientific version, *Sky Watching* by astronomer David Levy, co-discoverer of the Shoemaker-Levy comet.

**Astrology** is the art of predicting the future or interpreting events from the positions of the stars and planets and comes under the general umbrella of divination. It traces its origin back to the Babylonians. For the ancients, only seven planets – Mars, Mercury, Jupiter, Venus and Saturn and *including* the Sun and Moon – were visible to the naked eye and so early astrological charts assigned a planet to each day of the week. In contemporary astrology, however, Uranus, Neptune and Pluto have been added, and for convenience the Sun and Moon rank as planets.

Astrologer Ellic Howe wrote in the 1950s: 'The fact that so many people know their birth sign is a product of the mass-circulation newspaper and periodical astrology journalism that began during the 1930s. Those who have detailed knowledge of the principles of astrology almost unanimously condemn this 'popular' astrology as childish nonsense.' Nevertheless, despite its lengthy and fascinating past, astrology is alive and well, and expanding on the Internet. Obtain a reference book that is compatible with your own level of understanding of the subject. A title on my shelves is *The New Astrology* (Bloomsbury), which was a considerable help in writing *The Egyptian Book of Nights* (ignotus).

## Bible

The sacred book of Christianity, combining the Old Testament, the holy books of Judaism, and the New Testament, the books added by the Christians. The bulk of the present New Testament was accepted as authoritative by Christians c200AD; other Jewish books regarded as less authoritative, but sometimes added to the Bible, are called the Apocrypha. The most well known addition of the New Testament is Revelation or the Apocalypse, used extensively by horror-fiction writers for a good vs. evil scenario.

Probably not a title one would expect to see in a pagan library but it always helps to 'know the mind of the enemy', and a considerable amount of magical writing is bible-based. Fundamentalists of the anti-pagan fringe will always use biblical quotes (often out of context) when spouting their propaganda and again, it helps to understand exactly what they're banging on about before shoving the book back on the shelf. Of more interest to pagan writers are the uses of biblical references in Western Ritual Magic, the Qabbalah, and some areas of traditional British Old Craft.

## Correspondences

If we consult the encyclopaedia *Man, Myth & Magic*, the entry informs us that 'The lion, the sparrowhawk and the phoenix, the colour yellow and the number six, the heliotrope and the sunflower, gold, the god Apollo, a child, the zodiac sign of Leo, cloves, cinnamon and myrrh, a cock, a sceptre: the link which connects the items on this list together is the fact that they are all associated with the sun in ritual magic. These chains of association are part of what is called a 'system of correspondence'.'

For those well versed in the language of magic, it is easy to grasp how natural this language of correspondence (symbols) is, and how easy and obvious (in most instances) is the interpretation, because this language is made up of allegory, symbol and metaphor. Mystical truths that are concealed behind symbolic narrative; emblems that traditionally represent something else, and 'figures of speech by which a thing is spoken of as being that which it only resembles'.

Magical practitioners use many associations to aid them in their magic, with each area being assigned its own set of individual correspondences relating to colour, perfume, flora, fauna, gemstones, etc., and a thorough grounding in these enables us to evoke the right 'essence' for a particular working. It is often obvious why particular correspondences are assigned their place but many are equally obscure. The various different sources will all have their own particular attributions, although

Aleister Crowley's *Liber 777* has the most comprehensive listing.

## Dictionaries

A *Chambers* or *Oxford Dictionary* gives greater understanding of the *lingua franca* of the pagan community and helps give a clearer meaning to our writing; assists in the translation of the metaphors, symbolism and allegory attached to magical working; and strengthens the writer's own use of the English language. For example: we all know that the Latin *liber*, means 'book' but by consulting the *Chambers Latin-English Dictionary*, we discover that in Old Latin it referred to the inner bark of a tree that was used for writing on, and a code of civil or religious laws, i.e. the *Sibylline Books*. Liber was the name of the old Italian god of growth and vegetation, later identified with Bacchus, and the festival held in his honour on 17<sup>th</sup> March was the *Liberalis*. In modern Latin it is used to mean free, unrestricted, unhampered, open, unoccupied. And we now understand the context in which Aleister Crowley used the term '*Liber*' in his numerous writings, and not merely to appear clever by tossing in a bit of Latin.

*Brewer's Dictionary of Phrase & Fable* acts as an 'ideas' book that we can dip into and find all sorts of obscure references to the earliest use of terms from the writings of the Greeks and Romans, the Bible, Chaucer, Shakespeare and many others, through the poets and novelists of the Victorian era, together with a full explanation of mythic and literary references. The idea for my book *Aubry's Dog* (Moon Books) came from a suggestion triggered by an entry in *Brewer's*.

*The Dictionary of Magic & Mystery* (Moon Books) has over 3,000 entries and 26 mini-features that offer a jumping-off point for further research, while the *Dictionary of Gods and Goddesses, Devils & Demons* (Routledge) contains around 1,800 entries and covers all the important deities and demons from around the world. An old classic, *Dictionary of Demons* by Fred Gettings (Rider), has over 2,000 entries that help us understand the iconography of medieval, Renaissance and classical imagery. *Chambers Dictionary of the Unexplained* contains over 1,300 entries as a guide to the mysterious, the paranormal and the supernatural, while *Alchemy – An Illustrated A-Z* (Blandford) with its 500-plus entries offers an intriguing introduction to the subject.

## Encyclopaedias

For encyclopaedias focussing on the metaphysical and esoteric, the granddaddy of them all remains the 24-volume edition of *Man, Myth & Magic*, edited by Richard Cavendish. *MMM* was originally published as a British weekly magazine by Purnell and Sons; publication commenced in 1970 until 1972, continuing for 112 issues spanning 1,000 articles with some 5,000 illustrations, many of them in full colour. Purnell also sold binders for gathering the instalments into seven volumes, plus one additional binder for the magazine covers, and more than 200 academics and specialists contributed to the magazine. Now a collector's item, the full set can occasionally be found on e-Bay, Amazon or ABE-Books, although an updated version was brought out in 1994.

For those writing in the ritual magic genre, the must-have encyclopaedia is the ten-book *Equinox* vol 1 and the 'Blue' *Equinox* by Aleister Crowley, although *Gems from the Equinox*, edited by Israel Regardie, is available at a more realistic price. The original was published between 1909 and 1914, with one issue appearing every six months at the Spring and Autumnal Equinoxes of that five-year period. The companion volume, *Magick*, has probably been plagiarised and pilfered by writers more than any other reference book on the subject.

With more than 500 entries, *The Encyclopaedia of Witches & Witchcraft* (Checkmark) by Rosemary Ellen Guiley has been around for a while but is probably the most comprehensive as far as writers about witchcraft are concerned. A more academic source is *The Encyclopaedia of Witchcraft & Demonology* by Rossell

Hope Robbins. First published in 1959, this is still the most authoritative and comprehensive body of information about historical witchcraft and demonology ever compiled in a single volume.

## Folklore

The definition of folklore is 'the ancient observances and customs; the notions, beliefs, traditions, superstitions and prejudices of the common people'. And as folklorist Christina Hole points out, folk-customs range 'freely through countless centuries, and carries us back to our earliest recorded beginnings, and beyond'. In every culture, evidence can be found of surviving customs that can trace their ancestry a very long way back, not to mention those that appear to have vanished completely.

In writing for the pagan market, we need to be aware of the shift in dating that occurred when most of the world (in stages) adopted the Gregorian calendar in the 1700s. Although it wasn't until 1949 when China adopted the Gregorian calendar that the entire world could agree what the date was. As a result of these changes and the migrations from rural to urban, much of the people's folklore lost its old meanings and significance, while in more recent time many customs that had been allowed to lapse have been revived, largely due to the international lure of tourism.

Pagan writers learn to look behind contemporary recordings and analysis of folklore, and to see where attempts have been made to shake paganism loose from the customs. *The Penguin Guide to the Superstitions of Britain & Ireland*, by Steve Roud, and Reader's Digest's *Folklore, Myths & Legends of Britain* will both have the equivalent in other countries, but a book on native superstitions is essential for any pagan author's bookshelf. Frazer's *The Golden Bough* remains a classic for everyone despite it being part of the Victorian sanitation of international folklore, while *The Calendar* by David Ewing Duncan helps put festive dating back into perspective.

## Gemstones

Although shop-bought rocks and crystals are beautiful things to own, those with the greatest magical properties are the ones we find for ourselves. The traditional witch was more likely to use a local piece of rock (or pebble) as a power object or amulet, and most people can visit a shingle beach – where we will find a wide variety of colourful and beautiful semi-precious stones which are ours for the taking. Having said that, good pebbles are to be found anywhere in a shallow stream bed, on the sandy banks of an inland river, turned over in a ploughed field, even dug up our own gardens.

Gems and semi-precious stones represent important magical correspondences from birthstones to protective sigils for talismans and amulets, which are explained in some depth in *Magic Crystals, Sacred Stones* (Moon Books) and Aleister Crowley's *Liber 777*. We also need an illustrated field-guide, for example *A Field Guide to Rocks and Minerals* (Peterson Field Guides), that will explain the geological differences between similar varieties of crystal, gemstone and mineral. Or, if we are fortunate enough, a full set of DeAgostini's *Treasures of the Earth* magazines from the early 1990s, complete with the gem and mineral samples.

## History

In 1961, British historian E. H. Carr wrote in *What Is History?:*

The line of demarcation between prehistoric and historical times is crossed when people cease to live only in the present, and become consciously interested both in their past and in their future. History begins with the handing down of tradition; and tradition means the carrying of the habits and lessons of the past into the future. Records of the past begin to be kept for the benefit of future generations.

Regardless of the path or tradition we follow, it is imperative that we are fully conversant with the history of the period our pagan belief reflects. The student of the Egyptian Mystery Tradition must be familiar with the history of ancient Egypt; the Druids with Celtic roots and the Victorian revivalist Tradition; the Norse with the legends and customs of the Vikings; witches should have read Margaret Murray's *The Witch-Cult in Western Europe* (OUP) and Wiccans Gerald Gardner's *Witchcraft Today* (Magickal Child); *The Druid's Primer* by Luke Eastwood (Moon Books) and *Traditional Witchcraft and the Pagan Revival* (Moon Books) show the history and the urban myths that have sprung up around each of the different Paths.

We should also have a collection of general history books that give an account of the social and political elements of the times that have captured our interest – such as *Witches & Neighbours* by Robin Briggs (Harper Collins); *Britain BC* and *Britain AD* by Francis Pryor (Harper Collins), and *The Seven Ages of Britain* by Justin Pollard (Hodder & Stoughton)

## I-Ching

Although this ancient work has long been used primarily for divination for well over 2,000 years, it has also been revered as a source of Chinese wisdom. Probably the oldest book in the world, the *I-Ching* or *Book of Changes* is certainly one of the most extraordinary – it is believed that it gives astonishingly accurate counsel to the serious inquirer but responds with a random or even a rude reply to the frivolous.

Traditionally, the *I-Ching* was read by using a complicated manipulation of yarrow stalks, one of 64 possible hexagrams was obtained; the inquirer then consulted the appropriate section of the *Book* for the answer to the question in his or her mind. The modern method requires three identical coins, a pen and paper. The reading is set by the way the coins fall as either heads or tails and by consulting the table to see which hexagram the pattern refers to. The simplest version is *The I-Ching in Plain English* by George Hulskramer (Souvenir Press), which is now consulted by millions of people across the world. See **Yin and Yang**.

## Ben Jonson

Ben Jonson is a 17th century English dramatist whose masque – *The Masque of Queens* – was presented at Whitehall on 2nd February 1609 to curry favour with King James, who had written a book on witchcraft and was obsessed with the subject. The masque is remarkable for the wealth of dramatic detail of what ordinary folk believed about witches at the height of the Burning Times, and much more lurid than that used by Shakespeare for *Macbeth*. A copy of *Ben Jonson's Plays and Masques* edited by Robert M Adams (Norton) is an excellent source for quotations in pagan writing where irony is required. It also offers a glimpse into the mindset of the 17th century, which led to the witch persecutions in England, and the use of language for the period.

## Karma

Karma is the law of cosmic requital for good and bad deeds, and a central concept of all Hindu and Buddhist sects. The chief aim is the acquittal of the soul of its debts, which is achieved by successive rebirths until the slate is wiped clean. Karma is inseparably linked with the idea of reincarnation – no karma, no rebirth. The soul comes back because of karma, and the bodily form it occupies depends on the way it acquitted itself in its previous life.

In contemporary paganism, reincarnation is viewed as a form of everlasting life, while karma is negotiable. It is therefore essential that anyone writing on the subject, albeit a casual mention, should be fully acquainted with the true meaning of both terms and not use them indiscriminately. For an accurate view keep a copy of *Eastern Religions* ed by Michael D Coogan (DHP) and *Ancient Wisdom, Modern World* by HH the Dalai Lama (Little Brown) on the bookshelf.

## Thomas Charles Lethbridge

TC Lethbridge was a researcher, archaeologist and parapsychologist, and although his theories were largely ignored by the academics, following his death interest in his ideas has been maintained within the esoteric community. Lethbridge was a dedicated researcher who studied 'the occult' with what he considered to be a scientific approach and put forward some credible theories on hauntings, witchcraft, dowsing and psychokinesis. His book, *The Power of the Pendulum* (Routledge), documented his experiments into dowsing by means of the pendulum. The book was the conclusion to his lifelong study of the 'worlds of the unexplained and the occult' and as a result of his research Lethbridge concluded that there are other realms of reality beyond this one, and that the soul is probably immortal. A pagan writer's bookshelf should contain several of his titles.

## Myths

When in doubt, always refer to the *Encyclopaedia Britannica* because the information is based on scholarly research and not pseudo-esoteric writing, which tells that 'myth, folklore and legend is now recognised as a vital part of the development of the human race, rather than just a confused jumble of ancient cultural children's stories. It is also accepted that at the roots of mythology and legend is a kind of serious philosophy that was not random and which had its own peculiar logic, even if this is not rationalistic logic that sits comfortable within the remit of modern society.'

Again it is necessary to work through an irritating maze of analogies, allegories, symbols – all of which means making connections between things which outwardly and rationally are not connected at all. Myths that might, at first glance, seem merely products of childish fancy are very far from being merely fanciful; they are the means by which ancient peoples expressed their fundamental notions of life and nature. These enduring myths are the *actual methods* by which they expressed certain ways of viewing the 'rules of life', and which were brought into existence by the manner in which life was regulated in their society; the myths reflecting the morality according to the lights of their time.

When we talk about the 'mythology of Egypt' for example, we are referring to the whole body of Egypt's divine and heroic and cosmogonic legends, together with the various attempts that have been made to explain these ancient narratives for the benefit of *modern* thinking. 'The *real* function of these myths, however, was to strengthen the existing tradition and endow it with a greater value and prestige by tracing it back to a higher, better, more 'supernatural' reality of ancient events. What men have thought, all over the world and all through history, about the supernatural *is* important not only for what it may tell us about the Mysteries of life and death as the ancients viewed them, but for what it tells us about human beings today.' If nothing else, it reveals what we have lost!

Very early in the history of conscious human thought, the priesthoods awoke to the reality that their religious stories (i.e. those that concealed the Mysteries) were much in need of explanation. As a result, the popular versions took over and the esoteric became exoteric. 'The myths of civilised peoples, the Aryans of India, the Celts, Egyptians, Norse and the Greeks contained two elements: the rational and what to modern minds seems the irrational. The rational myths were those that represented the gods as beautiful and wise; but the *real* difficulties presented by mythology spring from the irrational elements, which to modern minds appear unnatural, senseless or repellent

(*Britannica*)' For that reason we need more scholarly reference books on our shelves, such as *The Oxford Companion to Classical Literature* (OUP), rather than more 'popular' versions regarding the Traditions that we wish to write about.

## Natural History

The reference books I use more than any other in this field are *Fauna Britannica* by Stefan Buczacki (Hamlyn); Cassell's *Trees of Britain and Northern Europe* by David Moore and John White; *Wild Flowers of Britain* (see **Plant Lore**) by Roger Phillips (Pan) and *Mushrooms and Toadstools of Britain and Europe* (see **Plant Lore**) by Edmund Garnweidner (Collins) to make sure I get the facts (including spelling and Latin names) right.

Needless to say if you are writing about pagan matters from other countries, then you will need to acquire natural history books pertinent to your own part of the world, while still bearing in mind the traditional associations of European witchcraft and folklore. An understanding of natural history is an essential part of any pagan belief, especially traditional Old Craft and shamanism, because a great deal of the divination, meditation, trance work, pathworkings and recognition is based on the location and behaviour of our local flora and fauna.

## Old Moore's Almanack

An astrological almanac that has been published in Britain since 1697, it was originally written and published by Francis Moore, a self-taught physician and astrologer who served at the court of Charles II. The first edition in 1697 contained weather forecasts; in 1700 Moore published *Vox Stellarum*, (*The Voice of the Stars*), containing astrological observations, which was also known as *Old Moore's Almanack*. It was a bestseller throughout the 18th and 19th centuries, selling as many as 107,000 copies in 1768 and is still published annually by Foulsham, giving predictions of world and sporting events, as well as more conventional data such as tide tables.

There are all sorts of almanacs published across the world – *Jewish Year Book* (1896–present); *Wisden Cricketers' Almanack; Canadian Global Almanac; The New York Times Almanac,* as well as *Farmers' Almanac, The (Old) Farmers' Almanac* and various astronomical and astrological versions. There is *The Nautical Almanac* (1767–present under various titles – prepared by U.S. Naval Observatory and Her Majesty's Nautical Almanac Office since 1958). *Kalnirnay* is a yearly almanac for all religions, wherein auspicious dates, festivals and celebrations of Parsis, Jews, Muslims, Hindus and Christians and others are mentioned in detail.

## Plant Lore

A vast amount of pagan writing revolves around the use of plants for their magical, medicinal and healing properties. In the past, medicine relied almost entirely on plants, and even today, many Western medicines are plant derived, although the surviving bulk of this ancient wisdom is contained within the 'wort-lore' and domestic medicine that has been handed down via traditional witchcraft and country family recipes. *Memory, Wisdom and Healing* by Gabrielle Hatfield (Sutton) is an academic study of the subject of domestic plant medicine that is not always sympathetic to the Old Ways, while *The RHS Encyclopaedia of Herbs & Their Uses* by Deni Brown shows just how many plants *do* have medicinal qualities. And no reference collection would be complete without the statutory Culpeper for a genuine 17th century viewpoint.

Plant lore wouldn't be complete without some reference to poisonous fungi, since Britain in particular has more species of toxic fungi than anywhere else in Europe and it is not a subject that can easily be learned from books. Or, as one countryman said casually over a pint, 'Eat half a death cap and it's not a case of whether you may die, but how long it will take you to die.' And there are also a few species of fungi that become more dangerous if eaten in conjunction with alcohol! Have a copy of *Mushrooms and Toadstools of Britain & Europe* (see **Natural History)** by Edmund Garnweidner (Collins) handy for when in doubt.

## Qabbalah

Whatever celebrity magazines may tell us, the Qabbalah (Cabala, Kabbala) is *not* a religion – it is a system of oral Jewish mystical thought that originated in Spain in the 12<sup>th</sup> and 13<sup>th</sup> centuries, although there are suggestions that it may have Chaldean roots that go back some 2,000 years. Later the word was used for Jewish mysticism and occultism in general. A considerable amount of magical lore that has crept into contemporary paganism has its roots in Qabbalistic philosophy, and for this reason it is necessary for the pagan writer to have a rudimentary grasp of the subject. Two books that have a simple approach are *The Hollow Tree* by Melusine Draco (ignotus), *An Introduction to the Mystical Qabalah* by Alan Richardson (Thoth) and Dion Fortune's *Mystical Qabbalah*.

## Runes

The use of the runes, the alphabet used in the Norse culture of Scandinavia and Iceland, date from the 3<sup>rd</sup> century. They are found among other early Germanic people, but it was the Norsemen who retained and used them well into the medieval era. According to *Magic in the Middle Ages* by Richard Kieckhefer (CUP), 'Whether or not they were originally and essentially seen as magical is unclear, but clearly it did not take long for them to develop magical associations.' Traditionally a branch was broken from a fruit-bearing tree and sliced into strips, which were marked with runic symbols but, unlike the Celtic Ogham, the symbols were not based on the Latin alphabet. *The Wordsworth Book of Divining the Future* by Eva Shaw (Wordsworth) is the reference guide I use when needing access to the meaning of the rune stones but there are several available that give more comprehensive instruction.

## Seasonal Celebrations

The bulk of pagan writing revolves around the 'Wheel of the Year' – the seasonal rites and observances that have been passed down through the ages. *Chambers Book of Days* (originally published in 1864) offers an entertaining miscellany of the folklore and history associated with the turning year. Presented season-by-season, month-by-month and day-by-day, it combines a calendar of folklore with information on celebrations and religious festivals. *The Roman Book of Days* (ignotus press) by Paulina Erina shows us that much of our holiday and folklore traditions are a remnant of the Roman occupation before the arrival of Christianity.

All Paths and Traditions have their seasonal observances and we need to work well ahead of the publication date to make sure our material is received in time. For monthly magazines we need to submit material six months in advance; for quarterly publications the deadline can be nine to 12 months ahead – check submission guidelines for precise information.

## Tarot

The Marseilles deck is the oldest, and the Rider-Waite the most popular, but it usually comes down to whichever one 'speaks' to you in terms of design and symbolism as to which Tarot deck to choose for your personal use. I use Crowley's *Atus of Tahuti*, although most people prefer 'pretty picture' cards that offer greater visual participation and soften the impact if there is a negative aspect to the reading. It's all too easy to read into the cards what you want to see, so never take a reading on face value. Although we should have faith in what we're doing, it should not be blind faith.

Remember that the future is not fixed; it is a series of

probabilities that can be changed to bring it into line with your own personal wishes. As Chrissie Sempers of the Raven Emporium wrote in *What You Call Time*: 'This is the purpose of divination – not merely to gain a glimpse of the future, but to ensure that your future is what you want it to be ... If you do a reading and don't like the predicted outcome, now is the time to change matters in the present, to bring about the future you do want. A further reading should be done asking simply: what should I do now to alter my future?' Most decks come with their own instruction booklet, but a simple guide to the Tarot in relation to the 'magical' Qabbalah can be found in *The Hollow Tree* (ignotus).

## Urban Myth

According to Wikipedia:

> An urban legend, urban myth, urban tale, or contemporary legend, is a form of modern folklore consisting of stories that may or may not have been believed by their tellers to be true. As with all folklore and mythology, the designation suggests nothing about the story's veracity, but merely that it is in circulation, exhibits variation over time, and carries some significance that motivates the community in preserving and propagating it.

The most common urban myths within modern paganism are: (1) Folk laying claim to antecedents to which they are not entitled – usually made some five years after the death of the well-known personality in the hope that no-one will remember whether they were part of the circle, group, coven, etc. (2) The publicity concerning Satanism in the USA generated the ongoing urban myth of 'satanic child abuse' that kicked off in the UK during the late 1980s. Although totally discredited some years later, it still persists in some evangelical and social care quarters.

## Vampires

The most popular and enduring fictional interpretation of the taking of a person's life-force, and perpetuated by numerous television adaptations. Vampires come in all shapes and sizes – although very few fall into the elegant and sophisticated variety popularised by England's 'purplest' literary community, The Gothic Society, where the undead were enjoyed as literary heroes. A genuine vampire can be encountered on several different planes of intelligence but with the single objective of draining the victim of all energy and ability thus *feeding* in the classical blood-sucking vampire way, i.e. draining the life-force from a victim. The *psychic* vampire is doing exactly this.

Some may ask if these creatures really exist and the answer is 'yes' and they are all around you; and 'no' they are not neces-sarily enemies – they can be people you know and care about. Think about it. How many times do you meet or visit someone and feel tired and/or exhausted while in their company? Or you may find being in their company hard work. This is because these people knowingly, or unknowingly, are draining you of energy. This is only one aspect of a psychic vampire and when writing for the pagan community, it is advisable to be fully conversant with this condition. The best reference works on the subject is still Dion Fortune's *Psychic Self-Defence.*

## Wikipedia

An invaluable quick-check source for dates, spelling of proper names, reminders, etc., but highly suspect when it comes to reliable information about contemporary witchcraft traditions. Excellent on the subject of historical witchcraft and personality details, but although there might be plenty of information given on the site, double-check with reliable sources unless quoting your source as Wikipedia.

## Xenoglossy and Xylomancy: Divination

The most accessible reference book for divination is Eva Shaw's *The Wordsworth Book of Divining the Future* (Wordsworth), which gives a comprehensive A-Z guide of all the different methods and techniques of divination. There are plenty of recommendations for further reading and a quick-fix reference for any pagan writer. Divination is the oldest and most durable of all the 'occult sciences' simply because it is repeatedly seen to give accurate results.

## Yin-Yang

A great deal of Eastern wisdom is based on the idea that all phenomena in the universe are founded on two opposing forces. Initially these forces were referred to simply as dark and light. Later, the terms were changed to Yin and Yang. Yin being the female, passive, flexible and gentle force at work in the universe; and Yang, the male principle characterised by decisiveness, activity, hardness and rigidity. All forms of Life, and by reason all the functions of the human spirit are associated with Yin and Yang. The Yin and Yang forces are at work in all processes of growth and decay, in the cycle of the seasons, in everything we do, think, experience and undertake. In fact, without the interaction of Yin and Yang, there would be no Life. See *The I-Ching in Plain English*, G. Hulskramer (Souveni Press).

## Zodiac

In astrology, this is a circle in the sky though which the sun, moon and planets appear to move, divided into 12 'signs'. A planet's position in the zodiac is believed to affect the way in which it influences people and events on Earth. The signs of the traditional 'tropical' zodiac are not identical with the actual constellations in the sky – the 'sidereal' zodiac. See **Astrology**. The 12 signs are arranged in a crude belt across the sky, completely girdling the Earth. Month by month, the Sun moves into a new 'sign' so that the astrological calendar runs as follows: Aries, Taurus, Gemini, Cancer, Leo, Virgo, Libra, Scorpio, Sagittarius, Capricorn, Aquarius and Pisces. The tropical system was adopted during the Hellenistic period and remains prevalent in western astrology, while a sidereal system is used in Hindu or Vedic astrology.

There are several type of zodiac in existence, with the most popular being consulted in the West as given above – and the Chinese zodiac. The Chinese star 'signs' in correct order are calculated yearly: as in the Year of the Rat, Ox, Tiger, Rabbit (or Cat), Dragon, Snake, Horse, Goat, Monkey, Rooster, Dog and Pig (or Boar) and are also closely aligned with the **I-Ching**.

There is also the Egyptian or Dendera zodiac, and although the Egyptians recognised the movement of the stars, they didn't adopt astrology until towards the end of the Empire. The zodiac ceiling at Dendera – with its star signs for the hippopotamus and crocodile – is Graeco-Roman and hardly Egyptian at all. The modern Egyptian zodiac assigned to the names of deities is a modern invention.

There is a lot of mystery surrounding Mayan astrology and the exact meanings of the 'signs' remains unclear. Many modern interpretations are available but few of them are based on genuine research into Mayan culture and the symbolism used by them. According to an Internet site: 'What is known is that the Haab Calendar used 19 Mayan astrology signs to represent the movement of the days throughout the year. Many of the meanings and symbolism are based on aspects important to their culture; weather, the jaguar, the four directions, and astronomy.'

Vedic signs are called *rashis* (pronounced = *raw-shees*) in Sanskrit, which gives the signs with their rulers, Sanskrit names and symbols, etc., and are the same as used in Western astrology. The interpretation of the signs, what they do, and the demigods who control them are vastly different in Vedic astrology.

Reference books are the life's blood of the writer and the more we use them, the more ideas they seem to stimulate. We look up the precise meaning of a word for one article and find that our eye is drawn to something else that provides the germ of an idea for something else. And the more we use books that are not in common usage, the better and more original our ideas will be.

➢ Remember that some old books, once discarded, cannot be replaced and somewhere along the line, we will regret parting with them.

## Interview: Opportunities For Writers at Dodona Books

**Suzanne Ruthven talks to Maria Moloney, publisher of Dodona Books, about the opportunities for writers on the subject of divination.**

**SR:** Divination is possibly the most ancient of the occult sciences and yet its popularity has never diminished – simply because it can be seen to work. Are you happy to receive typescripts for traditional methods of divination as well as more contemporary approaches?

**MM:** Yes we are. Angel divination and so forth may be the latest fad, but more traditional methods of divination such as Tarot, runes, scrying, dowsing, and palmistry are enduring and never lose popularity.

**SR:** Are there any particular subjects you'd like to consider for publication at the moment?

**MM:** Something unusual would be great, we don't have a book on geomancy, but other subjects we haven't yet covered are I-Ching, Ogham, Gemstone, Scrying, Feng Shui, Dream Interpretation (not a dictionary), and general 'how to' on divination. However, any form of divination would be considered.

**SR:** What sort of material or approach would automatically be rejected?

**MM**: We don't produce divination cards, so any ideas for card sets regretfully would be rejected. We don't accept colour books or books with copyrighted material such as illustrations of the Rider-Waite Tarot deck (commonly thought to be in the public domain and surrounded with legal problems). Anything that has been done to death, for instance, Tarot books that are straightforward and have nothing new to them.

**SR:** Have you any additional advice for potential Dodona authors?

**MM:** I would advise authors to ensure their manuscripts are well edited and structured with minimum well-drawn black and white illustrations, but better still with no illustrations and limited diagrams. Write from an original angle, something that grips the imagination and wants us to want to try it for ourselves. Try to avoid overly academic tomes, which have a limited audience. Shorter books are welcome from 25,000 words upwards. Try not to go above 75,000 words. **www.dodona-books.com**

# Conclusion

It should be quite clear from the above that although pagan writers can also contribute to the 'mind, body and spirit' publications, the reverse is often inappropriate – simply because the pagan markets usually require an informed element of practical magic and often 'religious' content. Nevertheless, we can also see that many of the mainstream women's magazines also include what are labelled 'alternative' articles, including folklore linked to modern festivals, holistic health, alternative therapies and healing, self-help, good luck charms, etc.,

While many of these ideas fall into mainstream categories, there is a sort of literary no-man's-land, which used to be called 'slip-stream' – two completely different genres merging to produce a coherent whole. One example is an article I wrote for the *Funeral Director's Journal* on the subject of pagan funerals. From that original 2,000-word article written purposely for the funeral industry, the full-length book *Death & the Pagan* was produced under a pseudonym to explore the different funerary practices of the various pagan beliefs in a way that would also be useful to members of the caring professions and the funeral industry.

Another was the popular *Root & Branch: British Magical Tree Lore* that listed the 35 species of tree that are indigenous to the British Isles, and which enjoyed a large number of sales via The National Trust and The Forestry Commission! Although the magical associations were included in the text, the whole gave the impression of folklore as opposed to witchcraft – although there were numerous 'hidden' references to Craft that were only visible to those in the know.

So ... if you wish to become a pagan writer and write for the pagan community, you might find your outlets limited. But if you are willing to study the craft of the writer and learn to hone your talents, you might find that by looking through a writer's eye that there are hundreds of markets that will accept material that may be pagan at heart but strictly mainstream on the surface. Even if you initially feel that there's nothing in mainstream MB&S for you, don't dismiss the genre out of hand. You may discover you're sitting on a wealth of material that could be re-slanted to sit quite comfortably within editorial requirements for non-pagan readers.

**COMPASS
BOOKS**

Compass Books focuses on practical and informative 'how-to'
books for writers. Written by experienced authors who also have
extensive experience of tutoring at the most popular creative
writing workshops, the books offer an insight into the more
specialised niches of the publishing game.